FAILURE WAS NOT AN OPTION!

A Test Case In School Integration

Johnnie Mullins Fullerwinder

authorHOUSE®

AuthorHouse™
1663 Liberty Drive
Bloomington, IN 47403
www.authorhouse.com
Phone: 1-800-839-8640

First published by AuthorHouse 7/22/2009

ISBN: 978-1-4389-6368-6 (sc)

Library of Congress Control Number: 2009906481

Printed in the United States of America
Bloomington, Indiana

This book is printed on acid-free paper.

CONTENTS

Dedication

This book is dedicated to my husband, John Arthur Fullerwinder, and my two children – Arthur Lamont and Tonya LeEll. By sharing my unusual journey in the field of education, my children will be able to have an accurate understanding as to how courage, determination, and knowledge can help overcome difficult situations in life.

Deep appreciations are extended to the former students and friends who have frequently asked me to share this story. Of course, retirement has afforded me the opportunity.

Acknowledgments

Writing a book, especially one that personally concerns the author, appears to be a lonely process, even though family members are present. There is no doubt about it. However, this process eases somewhat with contact of friends and colleagues.

Therefore, it is in order to extend thanks and appreciations to Alice G. Robinson, a college classmate and owner of *Alice's Educational Wonderland Child Care and Enrichment Center* in North Carolina. She provided valuable assistance in helping to edit the book.

Also, special thanks to Otis Alexander, Director of The Danville Public Library, who provided directions on how to publish my book and have it registered through the Library of Congress Control Number process.

Overview

Entering unchartered territory can present a myriad of uncertainties. Yet, this very petite, and spirited young female African American teacher dared to step out as a pioneer and become the first to begin a treacherous new journey in education.

This book chronicles the challenges met by the first African American teacher attempting to integrate the faculty of a large previously all white high school during the earlier stages of the nation's mandated desegregation of schools. The setting occurs in a southern high school in Danville, Virginia.

The book also captures some of the history of school integration in the city and surrounding area.

Introduction

"Cry…adjust…endure,
but failure was not an option"

It's red! Obviously surprised, the young female student whirled around and announced these words to the inquisitive look on the faces of her classmates. The words flowed spontaneously from her lips, as they appeared to resonate throughout the room. This scene occurred during the 1966 school year in a high school science classroom in Danville, Virginia, where the first black teacher added to the white faculty was conducting a laboratory exercise on blood-typing. Striving to generate interest and excitement, she had volunteered herself to donate a few drops of blood for the microscope slide that would be used for a demonstration. Eager to encourage direct student participation, the dark skinned African American female teacher had asked for a student volunteer to assist in the activity and come up to pierce her finger. The class of students just sat there for a few minutes, then one young lady slowly raised her hand to volunteer. When the teacher invited her up, she quickly walked to the front of the room, took the lancet given to her by the teacher then quickly pierced the tip of the extended finger. Almost as swiftly as she had pierced, the student stepped back and looked to see what would actually emerge. It was after a small amount of bright red liquid appeared at the teacher's finger's tip, her face registered a look of shock and she turned to the class of all white students with the announcement… *It's red!* To the teacher's amazement, it was obvious the students were expecting to see black blood ooze from the small cut on her dark colored finger.

This young teacher was me, Johnnie Mullins Fullerwinder, where I had recently accepted a teaching position in the science department at George Washington High School. Being assigned there made me become the first black teacher hired to integrate the faculty of this very large high school. The school, well known for its rigorous academic programs and school publications , was located in the southern part of Virginia.

Now, many years later, after frequent prodding and encouragement from former students and friends, I decided to share my story and its many unique experiences in book form.

Looking back, I see myself having been thrust into the role of a pioneer venturing out into unchartered and possibly dangerous territory during a turbulent period in history. With a vast unknown facing me and no printed guides to follow, I had entered this huge school as a petite, African American female teacher, five feet two inches tall and weighing 110 pounds. I was smaller than a lot of my students, shorter than many of the boys, and only a few years older than many members of the senior class.

To understand the significance and complexities of my story, an examination of happenings on the national and local stages in our country need to be viewed.

The timeframe was a little more than 10 years after

the federal government had outlawed segregation by races in the public schools of the United States to afford equal opportunity and justice for every child. It was the position of the Supreme Court that " separate educational facilities are inherently unequal."[1] In the United States at the time of this opinion of the Court delivered by Chief Justice Earl Warren, there were basically two separate societies, a white and a black, with each largely invisible to the other.

Despite this historical/landmark decision by the Supreme Court " *Brown V. The Board of Education*" in May 1954, it met with stiff opposition in most southern states that opposed the mixing of colored (black) and white citizens. The country was literally thrown into a long period of turmoil as resistances to this ruling harden.

Massive peace demonstrations were organized by those who sought to implement the court's decision to integrate the schools and violent anti- integration efforts were embraced by those who were opposed. There were basically two polarized societies, a white and a black.

Danville, Virginia had endured its own share of these negatives and sometimes-violent resistant efforts. During this period of history, Danville was highly segregated. The entire city was divided into two separate societies…one white and one black. Racism was prevalent. Danville was a city that took pride in billing itself as the last capital of the confederacy. It was not uncommon to see confederate flags flying from automobiles, homes and some businesses.

A tour of the city and its many streets revealed a common sight for southern cities: neighborhoods with residents all of one race; Separate schools, theaters, churches, mainly white

---

[1] National Archives. (1954). Brown v. Board of Education of Topeka, Kansas," 347 US. 483. Washington, DC: National Archives.

restaurants and theaters for each race. Then there was the very painful reality of some *"colored"* and *"white"*signs on public restrooms and water fountains.

A highly publicized Non-Violent March for Justice and Equal Opportunities for minorities had occurred in 1963 that resulted in many African Americans being seriously injured and thrown into the local jails.

Two separate, but highly unequal, school systems existed for the two races.

A short period after that painful March for Justice, a handful of black students had broken the race barrier as they were allowed to enroll at the all white George Washington High School in 1964. They had transferred from the all black John M. Langston High School.

I can't begin to imagine the harsh challenges each member of this very small group of black students (about six) must have endured as they dared to set foot in this very large all white high school. The city was still in the early infancy stages of dealing with the realities of integration.

Another school system in Virginia was so vehemently opposed to the Supreme Court order of integration that they chose to close all schools. Prince Edward County located about 70 miles from Danville had chosen to close all of its public schools in defiance of the court ordered integration of black and white students in the same schools.

It is against this unusual backdrop that my story begins as it focuses mainly on that unforgettable first year for me!

It was two years, after that small group of black students entered George Washington High School, that an African American adult was introduced into this arena as a classroom teacher. In 1966, I became that individual! I was the first one to walk out into this unknown and possibly explosive realm of teaching, as I would aspire to gain the acceptance of the students, faculty, and even more challenging the white parents who had never encountered this in their own upbringing and school experiences.

Having taught three years in another state, South Carolina, prior to coming to Danville, I was hired into the system at the beginning of the 1966 school year, unaware, to "test the water" for the acceptance of a black instructor in this overwhelmingly white high school. Not being a native of Danville, I had moved to Virginia with my husband, John, during the latter part of 1965 after the birth of our first child, Arthur Lamont. My husband had gained employment a year earlier in the adjourning school system of Pittsylvania County while I remained in South Carolina. He was assigned to teach in a black elementary school located in the county seat of Chatham.

Although an experienced teacher with three years on my résumé in my home state, it was still another southern state. Therefore, my teaching career had been in an all black high school setting prior to coming to Virginia.

I had been hired after college to teach science at my high school alma mater, Carver High School in Spartanburg, South Carolina. The entire school system there was totally segregated, as was typical of most southern states during this period of history. When I left the city there were still " colored" and "white only" signs on water fountains and public restroom doors. Restaurants had a small window usually located in a back wall to provide takeout orders for black customers. Blacks citizens were not allowed inside the establishments to order food or to eat. Two nationally known colleges were located there, but both had a closed-door policy that denied black students access to enrollment.

The city's all black high school, although totally segregated, had produced some outstanding graduates who went on to become nationally known figures.

Being hired into the Danville School System and assigned to George Washington High School was definitely a " first of its kind" experience for me!

The Hiring

I vividly remember, the job interview for a teaching position in Danville. An application had been submitted near the ending of the 1965-66 school year. This historic moment began with a telephone call from the Office of the Superintendent and an interview with the administrative assistant. This gentleman, who introduced himself, as Mr. Basker, was a very pleasant and knowledgeable individual. I was asked to come in for an interview the summer before the 1966-67 school year would begin. On the day of the interview and nervous over the prospect of being hired into a new school system, I parked the car in front of the city hall building where the school board office was located.

With my mind fixed on the interview, I walked right past the parking meter located on the street in front of the car and entered the building. Upon returning to my car, there was a parking ticket on my windshield for failure to put money in the meter. Suddenly, I was jarred back into reality! I don't remember even seeing the meter! Since I didn't have any money I had to go home to get money to pay the fine.

After the initial interview, I was called back for a second one. This time it would include the superintendent, who was introduced to me as Mr. Bonner. He was a very professional and serious appearing individual who immediately began to point out items on my resume with which he was pleased. Lots of discussion occurred around my philosophy of education. At one point during the interview, I was asked, if I would consider an offer as a school librarian, if no science positions were available. My response was no because my expertise was in science. During the conference there was a casual question of how I felt about students in general including students of another race. My response was I love teaching. In a classroom I see students, not color. After what seems like forever, the interview ended with the superintendent saying he thought they would have a position to offer me in the school system, but since the list of vacancies had not been completed he could not specify just where. Both gave assurance they would contact me later.

Leaving the interview feeling good, I was almost certain my assignment would be at John M. Langston High School (the black High School) where there would be an opportunity to make lots of new friends. With a college major in biology and a minor in the general sciences, it was really my desire to be assigned to the high school level where I could teach biology. If no vacancies existed at Langston, I had resigned myself to accept a position at The Westmoreland School, which was comparable to the current middle school organization. Westmoreland was close to where I was living at the time so it would have been conveniently located.

Several weeks went by after the interviews and summer vacation was approaching for my husband as the school year was ending. Having heard nothing else from the superintendent's office, I called to inform him of an offer just received for employment in the adjourning school system (Pittsylvania County Schools) where my husband was employed. Immediately he responded, " Don't sign a contract with them, we are working on a placement for you in the Danville City Schools!" He assured me a contract was on the way. My family and I were headed back to South Carolina for a few weeks to visit with our parents, so I informed him of this. He asked that I leave a forwarding address where I could be reached in South Carolina.

Three days after we arrived in South Carolina, the contract arrived there at my parent's house. It was very exciting when I saw the envelope with a return address from the Danville School Board Office. Upon opening the letter, it read "Your assignment will be- science teacher at George Washington High School." Immediately, I said to my husband, "this is a mistake that's the white high school." After some discussion, we decided the important thing was I had a job in the school system; verification of the exact site could be done later when we got back to Danville.

As soon as we returned to Danville, a call was made to the superintendent's office to verify the assignment. He was not in, but the person who answered the phone had the list of all new teachers and verified that my assignment was correct.

My husband and I immediately contacted a very nice childcare provider to make plans for her to come in and keep our baby, Arthur Lamont. He would turn one year old prior to my beginning the new job. She was a neighbor we had met earlier who lived across the street and had been attracted to the baby. I was pleased she would come into our home so the baby could remain in his familiar environment.

Feeling that Arthur would be in good hands, the emphasis then turned to the new job. I excitedly began to review books and teaching aids used on my previous job that might be of assistance. Not knowing the exact subjects to be taught, a variety of items were collected. Since I still didn't know a lot of people in Danville, there were few individuals to share the good news of my landing a job within the school system. My major contact had been with a family whose daughter had attended the same college in Virginia as my husband.

Coming in as an outsider to Danville, I knew very little about George Washington High School except it was the city's white high school. Thinking… well the school system has finally decided to place some black teachers at George Washington High School and I was going to be one of them. I was sure there would be other black teachers including some from the faculty of Langston High School.

I had never had an opportunity to visit George Washington High School for any reason, so was not familiar with the school. After receiving confirmation of my school assignment, I wanted to view the school from a closer range having only seen it from a distance earlier. John and I drove by the campus one Sunday afternoon for a close-up look at the premises. Taking this trip over, gave me an opportunity to familiarize myself with the various entrances and areas for parking. Since this was a weekend, our view was limited to the outside of the building. As we approached the campus, it was obvious the facility was much larger than imagined and very attractive.

George Washington High School was a beautifully designed red brick school lined with lots of windows and doors. The school, located on a spacious and well-maintained campus, resembled a small college. The front of the building was quite impressive with a very long cement porch and tall columns. There were several wings to the building that included an auditorium on the front end of the building and a gymnasium attached at the rear end of the building. Near the auditorium was a large parking lot designated for teachers. Several yards down from the gymnasium was a football stadium. Another parking lot was on the rear end of the school near the gymnasium. I was later informed that this lot was reserved for seniors, school visitors, and fans attending athletic events.

George Washington High School
Front of Building (Top), Back of Building(Bottom)

Meeting The Faculty
And Students

The Science Department

It was not long after that Sunday afternoon drive-by the big day arrived for me to report to my new teaching assignment. On August 29, 1966 off I headed to George Washington High School with a new brief case and a feeling of pride and self esteem. As soon as I arrived at the front entrance an assistant principal came up and welcomed me. I did not meet the principal that first day. The assistant led me down a long corridor to the science department. There he introduced me to one of the male teachers, Marsh, who was filling in for the department chairman. I was informed that the science department chairman would be away during the "pre-school conference" days due to a death in his family.

It was apparent Marsh was expecting me that first day. He extended greetings then went about introducing me to each of the other members of the department. There were 12 teachers in the science department that year. Almost half of them were new to the faculty just as I was. Some were friendly and others were reserved. The science wing was isolated from the other areas. It was far away from the main office located at the opposite end of the long central corridor. I was shown some of the rooms including where I might be actually teaching.

Each department of teachers held their own meetings during the pre-school planning days of a new school year. It was interesting to observe I was the only black teacher in my department. This was not a concern for me because I realized this was only one of several departments in this large school. I would have an opportunity to meet the black teachers assigned to some of the other subject areas when all departments came together at our first big faculty meeting.

During the course of that day, the teacher informed me of the various science classes to be offered in our department. Since a specific number of science courses were required for graduation, every student enrolled in the school would at some point have to take classes in our department.

Not actually being the chairperson, he did not delve too much into specific requirements for teachers in our department that school term. He did seem curious about me and spent a little time inquiring about my past experiences.

We were able to leave early, that first day, about an hour after lunch. All teachers were required to meet in the cafeteria the next morning for our first full faculty and staff meeting. It would be at this meeting that we would receive our teaching schedules and class rolls.

The Entire Staff

Filled with excitement and a high level of anticipation

for my new job, the next morning I made my way toward the first faculty meeting being held during the "pre-school conference" days. Eager to make a good impression, I reported a few minutes early to the school cafeteria where the meeting was to be held. The principal, Mr. Christi, was standing just inside the doorway. He greeted me for the first time as I entered the room along with three other teachers. Once inside the cafeteria, I glanced around this huge room. It had great lighting with several rows of very tall windows extending the length of the room on both sides. I observed several long tables had been lined up around the room to form a large rectangle for the meeting.

After speaking to some teachers as I entered the room (I don't remember any responses), I was directed to a section of the rectangle reserved for the science department.

My first reaction was to sit down and look through the packet of materials on my table. While I was busy doing this, the room was quickly filling up with other teachers and staff members. Two other new science teachers sat on each side of me. It was then I began looking around the room and received the shock of my life; in this huge gathering " *I was the only African American present*". The staff consisted of approximately 150 individuals, which included a principal, and two male assistant principals. The student enrollment, I had learned earlier was approximately 2,300 with grades 9-12, and here *I was the only black teacher in the room!*

It was at that moment, I developed a terrible headache that would last an entire month! It was like I had been struck by a bolt of lightning! Numerous thoughts began racing through my head, " Oh my goodness, is this reality or am I dreaming? Did someone forget to mention this to me? Was something said in the job interview that I missed? Where are the other black teachers I had expected to see"?

Throughout these silent discussions with myself, the numbness I felt prevented me from panicking or exhibiting any outward signs of fear. Inexplicably, I managed to hold myself together in spite of the pounding headache! Somehow, I was able to respond to those seated beside me in a polite and professional manner, as a colleague would later reveal to me.

Several new teachers had joined the staff that year; we were all introduced by departments and asked to stand as a group when our department was recognized. The principal then welcomed the entire group of new teachers to the staff.

Wow! To this day, I don't know if I would have resigned had I known what awaited me!

I don't know if the other teachers had been made aware an African American was being added to the staff. I hung around a few minutes after the meeting ended, but don't remember anyone coming up to welcome me aboard. Most teachers seemed eager to leave the room and get to their classrooms, I can only assume. Others developed conversations with fellow colleagues and avoided me. They either stood conversing in small groups or walked out together while involved in discussions with each other. The administrators were busy gathering left over materials so were probably unaware of what was happening. I was not the only new teacher, but my circumstances were obviously quite different from the others. Still half-dazed after this first encounter with the people with whom I would be working, I slowly walked out the door of the cafeteria and headed to my assigned classroom.

The Mysterious Restroom

Needing to find a small area to temporarily escape the stressful situation just experienced, my thought was to go into a restroom. I walked down a couple of halls looking for restroom signs that were labeled "white " and "colored" as I had been accustomed to seeing. After failing to find one and too proud to ask anyone, a decision was made to enter a restroom close by labeled "women".

Never having seen inside one of these "white" restrooms before, I had envisioned marble walls and brass fixtures. It was a slight disappointment when opening the door to the room. What appeared before me was a small room with plaster walls, a simple white porcelain sink, and a dark gray metal wall enclosure around the one commode. A simple round light fixture hang from the center of the ceiling. It was nice and clean, however. Inside, the small room were two other teachers. Neither spoke as I entered and said good morning. Trying to encourage interaction, I proceeded with some small talk about the large size of the school. Both hastily washed their hands and hurriedly left the room. I didn't generate any responses that day, but didn't stop trying.

During the remainder of that preschool planning day, time was devoted to working in my classroom trying to create an atmosphere that would be inviting to learning. Using my personal money, bulletin board materials had been purchased along with a few inspirational posters for the walls.

Not knowing what to expect for lunch arrangement, a sandwich and fruit had been brought from home to eat in my room that day. The school cafeteria would not begin operating until students arrived for the new school year. I didn't mind eating alone, because it gave me an opportunity to plan and complete some activities to be used with my classes. Since my room had a teacher's science laboratory desk with a water faucet, my hands could be washed and dried without having to leave the room. Besides, I would not have to risk another unpleasant restroom encounter that same day. The building was pretty quiet for a while as most teachers had carpooled and gone out to one of the restaurants in the city for lunch. No one had stopped by anyway to see if I wanted to join him or her for lunch. A lot of tasks were accomplished during this time alone.

Much later, one of my science colleagues, a male who was also new to the school and had come from a northern state, came by as the bulletin board was being completed. George asked why prepare a bulletin board? He expressed the view such tasks were a waste of time and his money would never be spent on trivia such as trying to beautify a classroom. It was his position the school should be responsible for funding such activity. The response to him, as I continued to work, was this effort helps to welcome my students to a pleasant setting.

During my previous three years, I had enjoyed teaching and witnessing student academic growth. Knowing and realizing that I helped in this wonderful process engendered a real sense of pride. So to me, it was unthinkable to begin a new year without attempting to create an inviting environment for learning to occur.

Bulletin boards all complete, my efforts turned to developing a few handouts and inspirational slogans for the five classes assigned to me. At the appropriate time, I gathered my briefcase and materials then made my way to the parking lot and my car.

Later that evening I went shopping for school supplies.

150 folders were purchased and one prepared for each student on my roll to keep copies of their graded assignments for parent visits and conferences. This effort would provide supportive documentation for all grades earned at the end of each grading period. My instincts told me this would prove to be a very, very, wise move!

That Evening at Home

That evening at home, a lot of time was spent rethinking my experiences up to this point. They had been so surreal. With a very young child at home, this was not exactly what I had in mind when applying for a teaching position in the Danville Public Schools.

I pondered the surprises that might still await me the next day after the teachers had an opportunity to go home and digest the day's introduction of a black teacher to their staff. Would the stand off continue? Would they embrace my presence or would I experience acts of overt racism from any of the personnel?

Since the superintendent had chosen to place me there and the year was just beginning, I chose to return to the school and my new job. Getting up bright and early and still somewhat stunned, I braced myself to face whatever the day would offer.

After those first two days, it wasn't difficult for me to find my way from the gymnasium parking lot to my room. This route was also much closer to the car. Using this entrance, it was possible to avoid a large crowd of people who would be arriving that morning.

Nearing the area, a light was seen in the room of the

colleague who had met me the first day. He was already there working, so I stopped by briefly to say good morning. Although in the midst of some paper work, he stopped to say hello and asked if any help was needed. Since I didn't know all of the school's expectations for teachers, I could not provide an answer. Noticing the paper work on his desk that needed his attention I soon left, but found the brief conversation to be uplifting.

No other teachers were in the halls on that end of the building, so I did not encounter any opportunities for negative experiences as I made my way to the room.

During most of the morning no one came by to check on me. Then about mid-day one of the men in the science department came in to explain the procedure for securing textbooks for the various classes. Teachers were responsible for reporting to a specific area to collect the books needed for their classes. I observed that he had brought with him a large wooden rolling cart. He then accompanied me to the room where the books were stored so we could secure the textbooks I would need for my classes.

Observing the stacks of textbooks, it appeared they were largely in very good condition and many were new. While slowly gathering books for the classes, my mind wandered back to the school where I had previously taught. The books used in the past were usually old, some almost falling apart, and had to be seriously taped together. I don't remember ever issuing a new textbook to students prior to coming to teach at George Washington High School. In my previous school, we usually received textbooks that were second - hand. They had been passed on to our school from somewhere else in the school system.

After collecting the number of books needed, the colleague

helped me push the cart back to my classroom and assisted in unloading the books. After explaining how to keep an inventory for the semester, he then left the room. It was very uplifting to have received the assistance. When he left, my attention was then directed to the preparation of forms that would be used with the book rentals.

Later, that day, another attempt was made to walk through a few of the hallways and try to interact with some of the other staff members. While walking, I passed several teachers and spoke as we approached each other. Some responded or nodded their head, but kept walking. There were those, however, who appeared not to see me although it was almost impossible to overlook my presence. No one actually stopped to engage in conversation with me or say welcome to the school. I didn't venture very far for fear of getting lost in this large building. After not being able to generate much interaction with other teachers, I returned to my room and remained there the rest of the day.

I still had not had an opportunity to meet the chairman of the overall science department who was away on leave due to the death of his father.

Introduction To All Teachers In The System
A Continuation of Meetings

Teachers, it seemed, were involved in a lot of meetings, prior to the arrival of all students at the beginning of a new school year. Before the week ended, a division-wide meeting was held for all teachers and administrators in the school system. The superintendent and school board members hosted this meeting to welcome teachers back and provide an overview of the new school year. All personnel regardless of grade level taught, school assignment or race, attended this very large "first of the year meeting". The site for the meeting was George Washington High School because of the seating capacity in its very large auditorium.

As the designated time for the meeting approached, I made my way to the auditorium. Just as I was about to enter the door, four of the other new teachers on the faculty approached and invited me to sit with them. They, too, appeared apprehensive about facing this large group of teachers. I sat beside a female teacher, Joanno, who was assigned to the English Department. Once inside the auditorium, there were lots of teachers slowly streaming in and taking a seat. Carefully observing this gathering, I noticed the teachers were largely grouping themselves according to race. This appeared to occur by choice, however.

After extending words of welcome to the 1966-67 school year, the administrative assistant to the superintendent introduced all new teachers hired into the school system. All of the new teachers were introduced as a group according to their assigned school and asked to stand for recognition. The high schools were the last to be introduced. As each school's name was called, beginning with the elementary schools, I didn't see any black teachers stand when a white school was called or vice versa. As the list was being called, from my point of view, I noticed all new teachers hired for each school were of the same race.

When the high schools were called, George Washington High was the last school to be recognized. The four other new teachers and I were sitting together near the rear of the auditorium and stood as a group along with all teachers new to GWHS. " *Once again, it appeared I was the only African American Teacher hired into a white school*". My colleagues didn't say a word, but I sat down stunned, with an icy feeling developing in the pit of my stomach! My ongoing headache began to intensify!

When the meeting ended, one African American teacher came up to me in the lobby and introduced herself as a faculty member at one of the elementary schools. She then asked me my school assignment to verify she had seen correctly in the meeting. She wanted to make sure she had seen me stand with new teachers hired for George Washington High School. I assured her that was correct as the expression on her face registered a look of shock. *Continuing the conversation with me, she wished me well and said I had made history in Danville.* It was very kind of her to stop and engage me in conversation, however, the remarks ever so sincere, did nothing to minimize my headache.

After that large meeting in the auditorium with all teachers ended and we were dismissed for the day, I had an opportunity to sit and reflect over the day's happenings. Although, pensive and somewhat stunned I knew the "biggest event" was still to come. In spite of all that had happened so far, I had not been introduced to the classroom setting. So even though somewhat apprehensive, I was still excited over meeting my students and actually begin teaching again. That very big and exciting event for me was about to happen the very next day. Full of anticipation, I braced myself for the unexpected!

Re-thinking my experience in the auditorium where all new teachers were introduced, I was somewhat puzzled. It was later that I became aware of some startling facts. Not only had I been the first teacher to integrate the faculty at GWHS, something more notable had occurred. The local newspaper reported another surprising observation, just a few days after students had arrived back for the new year.

The September 2, 1966 edition of *The Register Newspaper* reported, *"George Washington High School chalked up a first during the day. A Negro science teacher was present, marking the first faculty integration during the regular school year in the city's history."*[2]

At that point in time, it appeared I was the only teacher in the school system working at a school where the other faculty members were of a different race. It was probably best I had not been made aware of this earlier. *The news media never published my name, Johnnie M. Fullerwinder, but merely referred to me as a Negro science teacher.*

I was determined to always walk with my shoulders and head held high to exude an air of confidence. Never would I

---

[2] Register,The(1966),"New School Year Starts". Danville, VA: The Register, September 2, 5-B,5-1.

display any visible signs of fear.

Before classes would actually begin, there was an opportunity to meet the chairman of the science department. Upon his return to school, this gentleman whose name was Will came by to welcome me to the staff and offer help if I needed it.

Meeting The Students

The first couple of days for the new year, at George Washington High School, began with a shortened day designed for ninth and eleventh graders. Only a small group of eleventh graders actually showed up. The major goal of the one-half day sessions was to help orientate ninth graders to the very large school. This orientation session provided students an opportunity to navigate through the maze of corridors before the entire student body appeared a couple of days later. Once all students reported, there would be close to 2,300 students converging on the campus and filling the hallways. So on the first orientation day, all teachers assigned ninth grade classes prepared themselves to welcome this group of almost 600 students to their new school.

Teachers who were not assigned to any freshmen classes spread themselves throughout the building to assist with directing the students to the various areas of the building and to answer questions. Many of the teachers were assigned classes that were mixed with students of various grade level classifications.

The day was well organized with students first reporting to the large school auditorium where guidance counselors read alphabetical lists of students and their homeroom assignments. It would be in a homeroom setting that the official orientation would begin and students would receive important materials. Groups of students in the same homeroom formed a line at the front of the auditorium and were lead to their classroom by upper grade level student guides and a few teachers who did not have homeroom assignments.

Lists of the rooms and locations were later placed outside the auditorium to accommodate late arrivals.

I had always been adamant about punctuality and was usually in my classroom setting up for the day prior to most students arriving at school. It is because of this practice, on the first day of school most of the student body was unaware of my being there.

Homeroom

Since I was assigned to teach physical science classes the first semester, it meant interacting mainly with ninth graders for a while. Therefore, the first official contact I had with students that first year was with my homeroom class of ninth graders. The room I had been assigned for homeroom (S107)) was on the first floor and located on the side of the building near the gymnasium parking lot. It was a large room with good lighting and several large windows on the side facing the parking lot. From the room, it was possible to look out and see students arriving in their cars. Lots of students drove their own cars. Inside this room was a science laboratory desk located at the front for the teacher, two large chalkboards (one on the side wall) and a large bulletin board. Rows of student seats were neatly spaced to form a small aisle between each row. I had carefully spent time preparing the room for the arrival of my students.

George Washington High School (1966)
External View of My Classroom-S107.
Located on the South End of the Building

All of the ninth graders assigned to my homeroom were entering George Washington High School for the first time. An exception was the addition of a young lady in the special education program who was 22 years of age and would be leaving the school at the end of that first year. A practice at this high school was to assign a group of 25 or more students to a homeroom the first 15-20 minutes of each day. These students would usually remain with the same teacher during their entire high school career (Grades 9-12). This setting served as a nucleus of familiar faces, allowed school attendance to be taken, and general announcements to be made daily. Most of these students had other teachers for science and were only assigned to me for the homeroom session.

There were two African American students on my homeroom roll. I later found in this ninth grade class with an enrollment of 575 students, only 19 of them were African American that year. It was quite obvious; the school environment was overwhelmingly white. This made my presence on the staff more obvious.

A great deal of time had been spent the night before organizing important orientation materials to share or to pass out to these students. Teachers were required to purchase any extra teaching aids they planned to use in their various classes. To minimize the amount of personal spending, I had written the day's schedule on the side chalkboard along with a few other important tips for navigating the many corridors they would encounter during the day.

While anxiously waiting for my students to be escorted to the room, I heard a student guide outside my door announce this is your homeroom S107. The guide never looked in the room, but his voice could be heard. He then left to return to the auditorium and escort another group to their homeroom.

Upon entering the room, I cannot begin to imagine how stunned or angry that first group of white students assigned to me, as their homeroom teacher, must have been. It was obvious; my presence was definitely a surprise and not a pleasant one at that.

Already nervous and confused as newcomers to this very large high school, most never spoke as they entered the room in seemingly disbelief! It was obvious on facial expressions they were not pleased to be in this situation. Some sat down and turned so as not to have to face the front of the room. A few whispered to each other. Not only was this a first experience for me, it was a first experience for them as well. They had never encountered having a black classroom teacher prior to this historic moment. I tried to ignore the reactions and quickly went to work welcoming them to their new school and providing important announcements for the day.

Checking attendance was a requirement so I attempted

to call the roll. This effort did not generate much verbal response. Most of the students sat there apparently still stunned or angry over the situation because very few responded to the roll call and some of those were snappy responses. Since copies of printed class schedules had to be issued to each student, they were used as an alternate strategy for determining attendance.

Shortly after the roll call attempt, I explained that their printed schedules for the classes would only be given out during this special homeroom period. These schedules would be their only guide for assigned classes and maneuvering through the building. I then announced each student should come up for their schedule as I called their name. When the first name was called, the student got up slowly and walked toward my desk. While she was headed up, I then called the next name and kept the order moving quickly as a schedule was given to each student.

Upon returning to their seat, all students immediately began examining their schedules. A few turned to compare with their peers. Pausing for a few minutes before beginning the class, I was able to afford them a few minutes to engage in a verbal exchange with each other and compare classes.

After continuing my remarks, the attention was directed to the information I had written for them on the side chalkboard. The students probably assumed this was just standard procedure and did not realize it was a special aid prepared just for them. A few turned to view the board and others just sat there. It was my intention they would choose to jot this helpful information down in notebooks to utilize as they left my room. This did not occur, however.

On that first day, these ninth grade students were probably concentrating more on who was standing at the front of the room as their teacher than on any school handout or information written on a chalkboard. Hoping they would realize how helpful this material could be, I allowed the tips to remain on the chalkboard the duration of the first full week.

Thank goodness that first homeroom session was soon over and the students and I both could exhale. It didn't surprise me that at the end of the day, however, some of the parents called or visited the administration to request their child be removed from my class.

First Regular Class Period

After the bell rang ending homeroom session and signaling time to begin the first regular class period for the new year, an invisible tidal wave felt in my stomach seemed to increase in its level of intensity. As my first regular science class began that day, things were obviously different. A few of these students were sophomores or tenth graders who were repeating the course. One female student entered through the doorway, saw me, and stopped in her tracks with the comment…"*what*"! She then pinched her nose shut with her fingers and started to back out of the room. Someone pushed her back in; she hesitated and then slowly found a seat near the door. She sat there with her face flushed the entire short first period that day. I' m not sure she ever looked at me.

I found later, the administration, fearful of anything short of an all out riot when the students saw me, had assigned a male football coach, to stand outside my door as a visible reminder the school would not tolerate any disruptions. That coach later became my friend.

When the tardy bell rang, signaling time to officially begin the period, I turned to address the class. I quickly extended a warm welcome to the new school and another exciting journey in their educational career. My first remarks to students, after introducing myself, were "Welcome to George Washington High School. It is my responsibility to see that each of you leave my class at the end of the semester, a much better science student than the day you first entered. Your education has been entrusted to me and I take my job seriously. It is obvious that I am black, however, as your science teacher I have a lot to offer you. Whether you like me or not, don't let it prevent you from receiving what I have to offer you".

I could feel the tension in the room. It was so strong it could almost be cut with a knife. Seemingly, it was me against an entire class of students. I tried to appear calm and convey a sense of excitement as we prepared to embrace a new school year.

In this class, there may have been two African American students who were new to the school as ninth graders. They sat quietly appearing just as shocked as the other students to see me there in a teaching position. Apparently none of the students knew a black had been added to the previously all white faculty. I noticed these two students who had chosen to sit beside each other were being ignored by the other students, and just sat quietly observing the situation.

A synopsis of the course was given followed by a discussion of the basic materials needed for the class. I had prepared a short written assignment on their summer activities, if needed. It was pretty obvious the assignment would not be appropriate at this time, so I just talked for several minutes about the opportunities available at the school. Even though we were operating on an abbreviated time schedule, that period couldn't end soon enough for me.

As soon as the bell rang, the students rushed out of the room.

When all students had left the class, I had to quickly gather my materials and move to another room close by so that one of the other teachers could use my classroom.

As soon as I had gotten inside the room and turned to face the door, the next group of students was already gathering outside. A lot of commotion sounding like decision- making comments could be heard. Comments questioning whether they had to enter my class or expressions of them not willing to have me as their teacher. The tardy bell had to ring before some students would actually come into the classroom. Observing the looks of bewilderment and anger on faces, I ignored the fact they were entering after the tardy bell that first day. I felt this situation could be addressed later.

The students entered noisily, then wandered across the room to various desks and sat down. No one addressed me as they entered. A couple of boys argued briefly over the same desk and I heard another student tell them to just sit down. They then sat in adjacent desks. This classroom did not have laboratory tables, but regular student desks, instead.

The students just sat there staring at me with some frowning. I did not attempt to call the class roll since this was an orientation day. I also didn't want to deal with any situations that could encourage more disrespect.

Although each period brought a new group of students, my greeting and opening remarks were similar. I knew the importance of trying to set the stage for the remainder of the school year. Anticipating possible negative reactions and little student interaction, I had prepared a written assignment centered on their summer vacation to utilize if it were needed. I also realized some might not cooperate and do the written assignment, but at least it would be an organized class activity to help deflect the tension.

I decided to share information regarding the class instead. By the time I finished walking across the room and talking, the bell was ringing ending the class.

When this class left, I braced myself for the realization that as the word slowly began to slip out to other ninth graders my classes would present more of a challenge.

Just as anticipated, much later, one of the classes that would be scheduled in the afternoon presented a greater challenge than any I had encountered earlier. Due to a counseling problem in the guidance department, I was inadvertently assigned a class of about 80% male students this period. By then, I am sure they had gotten the word of my presence in the science department. Upon entering the room, it was obvious they were not going to accept me without a struggle, if at all. The students came in boisterous. Some chose to slam their notebooks on top of the desks as they slumped into a chair.

It was obvious frustration was being released over having me as their teacher. With this thought in mind, I decided to allow them this method of venting very much aware things could have been a lot worse. I did realize, however, the need to try to reach out to them and not lose control. As soon as the tardy bell rang, I greeted the students then began the class session, offering the same sincere greeting and remarks as had been given to the other classes. I just talked non-stop for a few minutes while slowly walking back and forth across the front of the room. Most sat carefully watching my every move.

When the roll was called, some students responded, but others did not. Matter- of- factly, I offered a glimpse of what would occur in this class and what helpful materials they should acquire. After realizing there was not going to be a lot of teacher-student interaction this period, I assigned a brief written exercise. It was written on the chalkboard and I provided paper for those who had not brought a notebook to class. Some students refused my paper, but accepted a sheet from another classmate instead.

Some reluctantly began writing while others did not. I didn't press the issue because at least the attention was diverted from me to them.

Time appeared to stand still as the short class period seemed to last forever! When the bell finally rang ending the class, it was such a relief for the students and me.

After those first-day classroom encounters, I was happy I had chosen not to be in the hallways at the beginning of the day as the nearly 600 students entered for the start up of a new year. It was best; students slowly learned of my presence in the smaller classroom settings.

One of the colleagues in my department would later confide in me that just the summer before my employment, she had engaged students enrolled in her summer school classes in a discussion of the possibility of a black teacher one day becoming a part of the staff there in Danville. The response of most, she said, was," *We will never accept a "n" teacher*".

Wow! What a shock it must have created for many of these students, when they returned to school that fall and found me there. Even more shocking was some of them got me for a teacher!

Looking back, I now feel the letter of assignment to George Washington High School was mailed to me in South Carolina to prevent prior publicity because the superintendent was uneasy over the reaction my appointment would generate in the Danville community.

Becoming the "first" was never my intention. In fact, employment in a predominantly white school was never a goal. It was as though fate was deliberately guiding me through unknown territory with turbulent waters as a test of my faith, courage, ability, and humility. I had really worked hard in college to prepare for a career in education. In fact, I was one of only three females in my graduating class who was seeking a degree in science. I never dreamed it would land me here. My original goal was to enter the field of medicine, but after serving as laboratory assistant in college where I was sometimes asked to cover classes for my science instructor, I had been encouraged to seek teaching as a career.

Surviving The First Day!

The first day finally ended and with a sigh of relief, I slowly gathered my materials to head to the car. Just as I started to leave the room, however, my department head came by briefly to see if I was ok. An un-asked question, however, may have been, "Can we expect you back tomorrow?"

My school day had ended! In the office, however it was a different story. I later found out the principal and both assistant principals had to stay around much longer that afternoon to answer telephone calls from parents. Once students had gotten home the main office telephone began to ring with concerns and complaints from parents.

"Undaunted and determined
I showed up the next day"

A couple of parents chose to visit the principal's office bringing their child, as opposed to calling. Many were relating the disturbing attitudes of their child who resented having been assigned to a black teacher. Some students had fabricated stories of things I may have said or done.

I will never know the extent of their conversations or what the principals told parents. None of the three administrators approached me directly with the concerns. They held a conference with my department chairperson, instead.

As soon as I arrived back at school the next day, my department chairman was standing outside the homeroom door and asked permission to come in and talk with me for a few minutes. Since most students had not yet arrived, we closed the door so none of them would walk in and hear the conversation. Beginning the discussion, he asked for my assessment of the previous day's meeting with the students. It was then he began to share with me some of the concerns the principal had asked him to address with me regarding parent contacts that afternoon. Some parents had demanded their child be removed from my class and assigned to another teacher. The parents reported upsetting reactions by their child over being assigned to a class with a black teacher.

One young lady had been intimidated because she had to sit beside one of the few black students in one of my classes. She had gone home crying and complained to her parents that she had a black teacher and this black teacher had made her sit beside a black student. This was so appalling to her that she wanted to be transferred out of the class. I assured him students came in and chose their own seats the first day, so I was not responsible for where she had sat during that class session. The position he took was the office just wanted me to be made aware of the parent calls and concerns. He felt most attitudes would improve after a few days of adjusting to my being there.

After the short conference ended, he wished me a good day, then left the room. I then used the few minutes left prior to the arrival of the students to organize all of my materials that would be needed for my homeroom students. They would be the first group to arrive that morning.

It appeared all of my homeroom students were present, but not necessarily pleasant. Two students spoke as they entered the room, but the others came in very noisy. They were definitely aware of me now. Deliberately ignoring my presence they sat down and immediately became engaged in conversations with each other.

As soon as the tardy bell sounded, the office intercom came on with a few announcements that got their attention. The minute the announcements ended, I immediately called the class roll. Some students responded, others sat there without responding. I just continued until all names had been called. Upon completion of the roll call, I said "okay it appears I am to report these absentees to the main office for today" and read off a list of names. It was then the students who had refused to answer the roll had to speak up and say they were present.

Greetings were again extended for the new school year then their attention was directed to the orientation tips, still listed on the side chalkboard.

In 1966, students were required to rent textbooks, so I paused to collect funds and issue rental slips to be used in their various classes. The noise volume rose while I was distracted, but I did not make an issue of it that day.

As the various science class periods began that second day, there were notable absences in my first few classes. According to one of the more vocal students, the guidance department was in the process of making some schedule changes throughout the entire school. It would not be clear to me, then, for a few days, exactly who had been withdrawn from my class rolls and who was really absent from school. There was very little improvement in attitudes as most students came in slowly, took their seats, and then chose to limit their interactions with me. At the end of the day, I discovered someone had etched the "n" word on one of the student desks and another had done the same to my large bulletin board. There were a few students, however, in my classes who did not show any reactions toward me, they just sat quietly looking and listening.

The young lady who held her nose the first day did return, but she sat rudely turned to her side in the chair so she would not have to face me. I did not acknowledge her actions in any way. It was best, I thought, to ignore her and not make an issue of the situation. She never talked to me, but through body language communicated she had no intentions of accepting me as her teacher. It may have been instructions from the main office that kept her attending. The counselors probably refused to change her schedule without a justifiable reason.

In most classes on that second day, the students moved methodically as they entered and took seats at random. With a few exceptions, there were no greetings to me as a teacher or acknowledgements of my presence. Some immediately began turning around and talking to each other. I attempted to get their attention in order to call the roll, but many kept talking to each other. In the first class that behaved in this manner, I simply dropped a large book, a science encyclopedia, on top of the desk. The loud noise caused everyone to turn around to see what was happening. It was then; I called the roll, and announced I was passing out a written class assignment.

The night before, I had decided it would not yet be an environment for a lot of teacher-students interaction. Therefore, I had prepared what I thought was a creative written assignment to encourage individual seatwork the second day.

During the following class periods, calling the roll produced a repeat performance of the previous day with most students preferring to raise their hand quickly rather than give a verbal response. I realized I would need to devise a method of assuring correct attendance while we worked through this rough adjustment period. In an attempt to set the tone for a regular session, I began talking of how exciting this course can be and how much I encouraged their participation for maximum learning benefits.

A short time into one class period, a young man blurted out "Do you believe in non-violence? This was a concept embraced by large numbers of African Americans throughout the country during the heated civil rights battles. I knew he was testing me. Not being able to anticipate what he or the others planned to do if my response had been yes, I stopped what I was doing looked straight at him and answered, "No," I do not. The class became extremely quiet and no further discussion on that topic occurred.

The orientation days seemed to speed by and the first official day for the entire student body arrived. It was not a modified schedule day, but rather the class periods were of the same length they would be for the remainder of the year.

Homeroom, on that day, was a continuation of collecting fees and passing out pertinent school forms. It appeared most of the students were prepared to pay fees on that first official day of the new school year.

During my first actual class for instruction that day, I announced that textbooks would be issued. Upon completion of this process, students would then be assigned a specific section of a chapter to begin reading. It was after this announcement, I invited the students up by rows to form a short line at my desk as I checked their paid receipts and provided a textbook.

The first student in line was a male, who refused to look at me, but balled up his textbook rental receipt and tossed it on my desk. He then crossed his arms and waited for me to issue a textbook. I looked down at the balled up receipt, then back at him and I just stood there with the other students in line and the class watching. After a few minutes he turned to look at me, I looked down again at the balled up receipt, that I refused to pick up and unravel, then reached around him to the next student in line, who had been watching. That student slowly handed me his receipt the correct way and I issued him a book. The other students in line each handed me their unaltered receipts and I issued textbooks.

After the third student in line received her book, the first student, still standing at my desk, reached down and picked up the balled up receipt from my desk, unfolded it then handed it to me. I took the receipt, without comment, and issued him a textbook.

Challenges Everywhere

The cafeteria encounter was only the beginning of numerous challenges I would confront during that year.

My First Cafeteria Visit

After completing a stressful third period, it was time for lunch. The school's schedule had two different lunch periods. No one in my department, I found, was having lunch in the school cafeteria that day. The few teachers, who had the same lunch assignment, had brought bagged lunches and prepared to eat in the Science office or the teachers' lounge.

I'll have to admit, I felt extremely nervous because I was not sure what I should do. Pictures of the white and colored signs flashed in my mind. This was definitely unchartered territory, in the south and certainly in Danville! There was nothing in the teachers' manual that addressed this issue. African Americans, "colored" people as referred to then, were not allowed in the all- white restaurants out in the city in Danville. There was no one around to ask if there was a "colored section" of the cafeteria? How do I get my food? Is there a small window where I should go that is reserved for "colored" people as it was out in the city. Do I stand at the back of the line and where do I sit? My lingering headache intensified as this decision-making process continued, but I was hungry and had not brought anything from home to eat.

Torn between sitting this lunch period out in the science office or going inside to confront the unknown of this major event for me, I inhaled and said to myself, " Be brave, since no one has specifically told you anything, act like all of the other teachers on this faculty". Holding my head up and pulling my shoulders back, I walked into the cafeteria!

Upon entering the room, it appeared even larger than the day of the first faculty meeting when I attended the preschool conference and it was now full of students. There seemed to be well over a thousand people inside and all appeared larger than life! About five different lines of students were spread across the room all facing the opposite end of the cafeteria that was the front of the room. While standing in the doorway, I heard a lot of mumbling and whispering from several students already seated and who were probably seeing me for the first time or finding out about me. Since my attire was professional, (a dress, shoulder bag, and high heels), it meant I was not a cafeteria worker.

As fate would have it, several steps in front of me, were two other teachers. I didn't turn to look at the students; instead I followed the two teachers to the front of the room where they entered a door to a room that appeared to be designated for the faculty. Still following them, I went through a special line reserved for " teachers only" and purchased my lunch. There were two African American cooks who almost dropped their large pans when they saw me come through the line. They were obviously shocked!

As I sat down at the nice tables with my tray, an attempt

was made to engage people seated nearby in conversation. The effort produced polite, but brief responses! A few teachers apparently ignored my presence and never turned to look in my direction the entire time I sat at the long table with them. Other teachers were not rude, just very quiet. Realizing this was a new experience for them also; my attempts to engage anyone else in conversation during this first encounter were few! I don't remember what the meal was that day or even if I enjoyed it. I stayed only long enough to consume what I had purchased then left. I was relieved after I left, but felt proud of the fact that I had actually gone and had chosen an attempt to interact with my colleagues rather than give in to fear.

Having completed my first lunch in an integrated cafeteria was definitely an adjustment for me. With this challenge behind me, however, I was certain there would still remain many stressful experiences ahead.

Gaining Students' Acceptance

This was actually my second week of employment, but the first full week for the entire student body. It was about the third day of that week, following roll check; I explained we were going to use a special seating arrangement in order to help me learn names quickly. It would also aid me in being able to correctly record attendance. I would be able to look at an empty desk and immediately determine who was absent. An alphabetical seating chart would be used, it was announced. Some students immediately yelled out they wanted to keep the seat they had chosen. I assured the class this arrangement would benefit them in the long range, so we were going to try it for at least the first six weeks. If at the end of this time period there were still concerns, we would make any requested changes.

There was some grumbling heard throughout the room and a few snide remarks of not sitting anywhere they didn't want to sit. I proceeded to organize the seating chart and reassured them we would revisit this at the end of the first six weeks, if they still had concerns. Some gathered their books when asked to move to a new seat, and slammed them down on top of the newly assigned seats in an act of anger as they slumped down in the new seat.

Since I knew from my past teaching experience this was a very wise move, I did not give in, but proceeded with this seating chart assignment in all classes that day. Having them move around to different seats helped to occupy some of the instructional time and was an aid in helping to speed up the class periods for the day.

During the remainder of that week and the next one, I never mentioned my race or color because that was obvious to everyone. In spite of this, I experienced numerous instances of both subtle and blatant acts of prejudice.

Homeroom classes were still undergoing an adjustment to having me assigned as their teacher. Students were doing everything possible, it seemed to minimize direct contact with me. There was virtually little interaction between us. Most appeared to simply just go through the motion of paying for textbooks and various fees required by the school when having to come up to my desk. Usually students, after being assigned lockers, experience difficulty in operating the combination locks attached to them. I knew this would be an opportunity for interaction to occur, as I would help with operating the locks. It was surprising to note, however, after volunteering to help, the students preferred to ask each other for assistance instead.

I made it a daily practice to offer aid in helping make the transition from junior high to the high school setting, a smoother one. Some days, after the office announcements had ended, I would simply point to the chalkboard where I had listed helpful hints for that day.

Since students were not verbalizing their feeling, I observed actions and attitudes. In one of my regular science classes there appeared to be a decision not to participate or cooperate. Their actions were interpreted as, "we are only attending this class because we have to, but don't expect us to respond to you." In spite of their reactions, I continued to introduce each day's lesson just as had been done in my other classes. With persistence, the students gradually began to respond to written assignments.

There were a few students who never actually looked at me during the entire period or would sit with their head turned to the side. I sensed that some of them were not being encouraged at home to be receptive of me as a teacher. It was early on in the class the students were told, although I could not make them like me, they would respect my position as a teacher! I was going to do all I could to make them better science students by the end of the semester.

I had a very strong affinity for teaching and learning and set out to be the best possible teacher any student could want! In my mind, they were just students, but most of them saw skin color! I had to remind myself that out in the city and its various communities, "segregation" was currently the order of the day.

Shortly after my hire, there had been a Ku Klux Klan (KKK) Rally held close by in the county during the first week of September, according to the local newspaper. It was not clear if the rally was held as a protest against school integration, which included me. It revealed, however, the mind set of at least some white citizens in the area who were not ready to embrace black citizens. At that time, there were no black leaders sitting on a governing body; the city had never elected a black person to city council.

In an outside environment such as the one that existed, it became apparent, a major effort would be required to change minds of students and gain acceptance as a teacher. I definitely had my work cut out for me.

Adjustment with the teachers was not without its challenges either. Visits to the restrooms were often repeat performances of my first visit. After that first faculty meeting and the unpleasant experiences that followed during the week, I didn't spend a lot of time in the hallways. It didn't take me long to notice many teachers would still pass by me and look the other way or behave as though I was invisible. The corridors were wide so this was not difficult to do, if an individual wanted to do so.

The reactions were different with members of the science department, however. It was not difficult to generate conversations with those colleagues when I came in contact with them, although it was sporadic during the course of a day. With different teaching schedules and many bringing bag lunches from home, I did not see some of my science colleagues during the day.

The very large size of the building was intimidating enough as I struggled to get a handle on its layout. I always remained on the very large first floor area with its numerous dividing hallways. Located on this floor were the main academic classes, the office, guidance department, library, faculty lounge, cafeteria, auditorium, and the gymnasium.

"The bumblebee can't fly,
No one told the bumblebee,
So he flies anyhow"
Anon.

Special effort was directed to avoid being in the halls during the change of classes where there would be very large numbers of students pushing their way through to the next class. Many of these students did not have direct contact with me because they were not assigned to any of my classes. I wanted to avoid any potential negative encounters with them.

While outside the somewhat protective arms of the science office, there were many times I would feel so alone. It was often I would experience first- hand the meaning of an expression "feeling alone in the midst of a crowd". I was teaching in a huge institution with hundreds of people surrounding me for long hours on a daily basis, yet not really a part of them. The interactions that would normally occur with members of a group were not happening.

During these times, it became painfully clear that acceptance does not automatically come with physical admission to a building. The Supreme Court's order to integrate, while mandating the right to share the same space, did not automatically translate into an order to embrace another individual's presence. Special efforts it, seemed, must be exerted to make that happen.

Being accepted as an equal would require more than just opening a door through which one could enter. Entrance and acceptance were not always sequential actions.

There were times I would pose the question to myself, "why did fate choose to place me here"?

A phenomenon I heard in one of my college science classes was " according to the laws of aerodynamics the bumblebee should not be able to fly"…the odds are against it. The disproportionate wings to body size would lead to an expectation that the ability to engage in flight would be impossible for this insect. However, in spite of the laws and the seemingly impossibility, the bumblebee bucks the odds as it flies anyway. People, too can transcend expectations and defy incredible odds.

I was faced with what appeared to be insurmountable odds… treading in un-chartered territory, with no guidelines given, and nobody knowing what advice to give me because nobody had seen it done there before! I was attempting to be an effective science teacher in an environment in which a large number of the students simply resented having a black person in a position of authority. There were those who seemed determined not to accept me as a teacher. Many of these students, I was to learn later, had only associated with black adults in a position of hired service.

I did not want to become engaged in a battle, but if this was inevitable, I was determined to win…I had much more at stake than they! I was responsible for the educational progress of a very large group of students. They were not going to be academically crippled because of my inability to deliver. I was determined that my students were going to learn; I would strive to help ensure academic success for each one in my science classes.

To say I was not nervous would be less than truthful, with me being greatly outnumbered and not surrounded by any other African American adults, if things turned violent. Having been described by my husband as an individual possessing strong willpower, however, there was a determination to stand my ground. Since my role was designed not to harm, but to offer help, I would assume the same determination and defy expectations just like the bumblebee.

During those first few weeks, concerted efforts were devoted to reaching out and trying to gain the acceptance of my students. It was not an easy task. Although a few students would enter and extend a brief greeting, the majority definitely did not exhibit this action. In many instances, I received curt responses when directing a question to a student. Others sat guardedly observing my every move. I could see their eyes carefully examining every aspect of my outward appearance from my head to my feet as I moved around the room. It was a practice I had of never remaining at the front of the class, or in one spot, an entire class period. I constantly moved around the room when I talked or when I had students engaged in a written assignment.

At the school where I had previously taught, it was customary for female teachers to wear high heel shoes; a practice I continued at George Washington High. Students took note of this because I often saw them observing my shoes. This apparently was not done by a large number of teachers at my current school assignment.

Classroom Assignment

That first year, the classes assigned to me were physical science and biology. Most of my students were largely freshmen and sophomores. During the following semesters, as my teaching assignment was expanded, several juniors and seniors were added to my class rolls.

The room assigned to me for homeroom at the beginning of each day was on the south wing of the building, Room

S107. It was located near the gymnasium. The room was designed for teaching science classes which I was certified to teach. I thought it was very odd, however, that I was only assigned to be in the room just two periods and one of them was a non-teaching period- homeroom.

That first semester my assignment was to be a floating teacher who would require a rolling cart to move around to other classrooms, while another teacher came in to use Room S107. When questioning the arrangement I was told tenured teachers were given preference for room assignments prior to newly hired ones. There was a possibility; my situation could change the following semester, depending on the courses assigned.

As a floating teacher, one classroom to which I was assigned had poor lighting. There were no small tables for student group work, either. The room always appeared to be dimly lit and the use of optical equipment such as a microscope was not as effective as in other rooms. There were individual student desks with the tops tilted upwards, making it difficult to use much of the laboratory equipment regularly used in my other classes. I never felt small group work in this room was as effective as in some of the other classrooms.

With several rows of student desks, the room always seems too small to accommodate the thirty students included on my class rolls. The closeness of student desks provided numerous opportunities for distractions to occur. This arrangement gave me additional reasons to remain alert for any attempts at creating disruptions. Although the room was not really designed for science classes, the large student enrollment in the department made it necessary to schedule a few classes there.

A couple of foreign language classes were taught in the

room at other periods during the day. Its design could easily accommodate classes in most of the other subject areas, but it just did not lend itself well to the special needs of science classes.

It was a relief not to have more than one semester in that environment.

Eyes and Ears were Everywhere, It Seemed!

Although I taught behind closed doors, what went on in my classrooms was well known throughout the school. Eyes and ears were everywhere, it seemed, observing my classes daily during that first semester. Various indicators began surfacing to suggest this.

Son of The Superintendent's Assistant

In checking my class rolls, I received an unwanted surprise. Looking closely at the list, I discovered the son of the superintendent's administrative assistant had been assigned to one of my ninth grade physical science classes. Upon discovering his name, my stress barometer was elevated! I felt this might have been deliberately arranged as a way of monitoring my teaching and acceptance by the students. The positive side was the young man was cooperative and a good student academically. I'll never know what "behind the scene" influence he may have had on his peers. His class met in the afternoon, so he may have witnessed the less than pleasant encounters of my first day.

It wasn't clear whether the other students knew of the connection his father had with the school board office. They accepted him seemingly as just a regular guy. Maybe he didn't want to be singled out. I never knew for sure. Not wanting to make him uneasy, I never mentioned that I knew who his father was. He was a model student while in class never attempting to show off or flaunt his knowledge. Instead, he presented himself as a quiet young man who was responsive to my questions when directed toward him.

Classroom Next Door To Department Head

Upon discovering I would be teaching a class next door to the department chairman, I knew there would always be a need to remain alert. There was actually a door on one of the inside walls of my class that opened directly into his classroom where he taught physics classes. He could literally hear everything that transpired in my class. Both rooms were located on the end corner of separate hallways that joined together at a point similar to an inverted "L". Additionally, on the outside wall of each room were rows of large windows that could allow us to look into each other's classroom.

There were a few occasions in which he, Will, would use this inside door to cut through my classroom to enter the outside hallway that led to the gymnasium. A few other teachers would periodically use my room to access the hall leading to the cafeteria or the gym.

I was especially vigilant in keeping that class actively engaged in the learning process. Whether this class arrangement was deliberate or not I don't know.

Coach Stationed Outside My Classroom

The athletic coach, who had been stationed outside my homeroom door on the very first day of the semester, had shared his experiences with my department head and the administration, I was to find out later.

Teachers were Questioning Students About My Classes

While engaged in a conversation one afternoon with one of my colleagues in the science office, she shared with me some things that had occurred in my classes. Specific activities were mentioned. She even repeated the remarks extended to my students on the first day as I welcomed them to the new school.

A Substitute Discussed My Lesson Plans With My Department Chair

During the middle of the semester, I had to be absent for a day after contracting a stomach virus that seemed to be circulating throughout the school. Detailed written plans were provided for the substitute. They included roll check at the beginning of the class. The substitute who was an elderly white gentleman scrutinized the plans and formed his assessment of them. Later, he had openly criticized the plans in front of my department chairman while seated at the lunch table in the cafeteria. Other teachers were present and heard his comments. According to the substitute, the plans were too organized and did not need to include roll check.

The department chairman came to me the next day to share the incident and the response he had given. He had informed the substitute my plans were in the desired format. The administration, he said, would prefer plans of this type to reduce many unneeded problems they have to deal with when teachers were absent. It was noble of Will to share the incident with me.

I thought, "Even substitutes are reviewing and analyzing my work here!"

Enhancing Instruction

A lot of time was spent thinking of ways to enhance instruction and heighten student interest in science. Portions of my planning period were devoted to assessing the types of instructional equipment available for classes. Initially, two different days were devoted to carefully exploring the storage sites that housed science instructional equipment and teaching aids. Since these rooms were all located on what was classified as the science wing, I did not have to venture far.

The first visit to this area was an eye opener for me! Touring the various storage sites of supplies, I was simply amazed at the difference in quantity and quality of equipment here as compared to my previous school. At Carver High, there had been approximately five microscopes in the entire building because we were told funding was not available from the Central Office to purchase more. The teachers there had learned to be creative, however, and did more class demonstrations with students observing.

At George Washington High School there were enough

microscopes for every two students per class during any laboratory activity. Students were fortunate to be able to work in small groups of twos during the class period. In the past, I remembered setting up microscopes at various stations and allowing students to rotate around the room to observe the slides I had prepared for observation.

Looking around this storage area, I observed, there were several small cabinets with trays of prepared slides containing microscopic organisms. In addition, there were several small boxes of plain glass slides and cover slips.

Neatly standing at the rear of the room, were several life-size plastic models of plants and animals. There were large barrels of preserved frogs, earthworms and other small animals for student dissections. I saw, and later worked with so many large barrels stuffed with crayfish preserved in liquid formaldehyde; it turned me against eating shrimp for a while. On one large shelf there were several jars of preserved organs, tiny animals, and plants for classes to use. A small octopus, squids and stingrays were even among the collections in a corner on the floor.

In the past, I had collected some specimens from farmers who were processing animals for slaughter. The farmers were located in rural areas outside the city limits of my former school. These donated specimens were then carefully washed and placed in jars of alcohol. At other times, with permission from the administration, my classes had gone on short field trips near the campus to collect insects, small plants, and various leaves. A closer look around the room revealed several large flip charts of human anatomy, plants, and animals suspended from metal stands that could be transported to the various classrooms.

As I walked through the storage rooms, I was in awe! The volume and quality of teaching aid, supplies and science laboratory specimen almost equaled that of my undergraduate college experience. I had attended college in the state of North Carolina. Also, the high school in that same state where I had done my student teaching did not have nearly the volume of instructional aids I saw at George Washington High School.

As I went from one storage area to another, it was a great sight to walk through the classrooms and observe the rows of laboratory tables in the biology, chemistry, and physics areas. There were shelves of test tubes, beakers, flasks, other glassware, and various laboratory chemicals.

I had never seen so many glass beakers and test tubes in a school as the ones lining the shelves of the chemistry stock room. There were all types of weighing scales. Single and triple beams balances were available in quantities for small group work. Having direct access to this large volume of equipment and material would make teaching a lot easier, I surmised. I would miss being able to take my classes on field trips where we would collect our own items for study, however. With this inventory of teaching aids, there was no longer a need to actually collect insects, leaves and water from small ponds, as I had been accustomed to doing. It was as though everything here came purchased and pre-packaged for the instructional process. Some of the fun would be missing, but I had more options.

With total amazement, I left the areas thinking, "Oh my goodness, I can't believe this much teaching aid is available for my use!" I hope the students realized how fortunate they were to be attending this well equipped school. After this wonderful discovery, I knew many return trips would be made to the area. Adding to the excitement, I found additional materials, including small live specimens, could be ordered throughout the school year.

Near the end of the second week of the school year, it appeared the shock of my presence had worn off. The reality of actually having a black teacher was materializing in acts of resistance. All but one of my classes were exhibiting signs of resistance to being assigned to a black teacher. Not only did these students enter the room talking loudly, ringing of the tardy bell signifying the beginning of the class period, meant nothing to some of them.

Determined to succeed at being able to conduct classes conducive to learning, I found it necessary to become more forceful in assuring order. If I could maintain an orderly environment, I was certain I could do the required teaching. So being acutely aware of the significance of good classroom management skills to help foster academic success, I became very firm and would not tolerate any unruliness.

One of my colleagues told me the word was spreading among students that I was pretty strict. To me, it was essential to have order prior to any meaningful instruction to occur. After the first couple of weeks, even in a school setting with no one to come to my rescue if I needed help, I accepted no nonsense from students.

By the end of the third week of school, I had succeeded in gaining control over the classroom as far as assuring that students enter quietly and in an orderly manner. I was operating the way I had done previously as a classroom teacher. Students knew to cease any small group talking after the tardy bell rang. I would stand at the door to greet those classes that were more of a challenge and pass out a written assignment as soon as they entered. The assignments were graded for class credit. While they were working, this temporary diversion gave me a chance to get the class under control.

When a student talked across the room or ignored my speaking to him or her, I would stop what I was doing, walk within close proximity to them, stop and look at them with a raised eyebrow. This would get the entire class's attention, which usually caused the student to conform to proper classroom behavior.

The students were reminded that my behavior expectations were the same as those of the entire school system. Students were expected to conduct themselves in a manner that would provide a good learning environment for everyone. It was difficult for anyone to argue with this position. Students soon realized my classroom would not be a playground!

I quickly earned a reputation of a "no-nonsense" teacher who was "firm", but fair. My actions and behavior were directed toward being highly professional and respectful of the rights of others; the same was expected of them.

In the weeks that followed, the major problems I had to deal with in my classes were not typical problems of noisiness because I pretty much had that under control. Instead they were those intangible ones like the coolness in the atmosphere when I came near some students. There were those subtle acts of turning away when I spoke to one of them as though I had not said anything. The shrugging of shoulders instead of answering me when I asked a question, the condescending looks when I came near some or failing to refer to me by name to get my attention. A few students would preface a question with, "Hey, what did you say we were to do?" rather than " Mrs. Fullerwinder, what, are we to do?" When these instances occurred, I would stop and remind the student of proper classroom etiquette in addressing an instructor.

One young lady in a morning class was particularly resistant to my efforts to reach out to her. We never had a verbal confrontation, however, during an independent seatwork assignment, I was walking around the room checking students' progress and stopped at her desk to compliment the beautiful work she had done. After paying the verbal compliment, I gently placed my hand on her shoulder smiled and said, "keep up the good work". As I touched her, she pulled away from me, and never looked up. I just moved on to the next student to check his work.

As I pressed onward with teaching, the thought surfaced that even though the students disliked having a black teacher, these 9th graders were faced with an even larger threat I soon realized could be used to my advantage. They were filled with intimidation and nervousness of this very large new school they were entering with over 2,300 students and 150 staff members. It looked like a college campus. Additionally, some of the upper class students were pulling pranks on them. The school layout could be very intimidating (it was to me) with two large floors of several branching hallways and separate buildings on campus with no signs directing them to a specific area. They were also experiencing the concept of a different teacher for each subject for the first time and having to change classrooms at the end of each period.

On some days, a few minutes in various classes would be devoted to addressing school concerns of the students. How to successfully manipulate locks on their individual lockers in order to quickly make stops between classes was a common concern. There were also days I would take a few minutes to re-emphasize an important school announcement or re-iterate adjustment tips to help smooth the transition from their previous school experiences to the current high school environment.

All Challenges Did Not Disappear

Between my regular classes and homeroom sessions, many challenges remained. I still witnessed some instances of hardcore resistance throughout the school year.

While I was making progress with some classes, there was one afternoon class that consumed a lot of my energy. Among this group of students were some upper classmen who had failed the previous semester and were repeating the class. It was obvious from day one of the semester they were going to be a competitive bunch; responses to me were deliberately sarcastic.

The class, consisting largely of male students, finding their schedules would not be changed so they could be assigned to another teacher, refused to do much work in my class. I found racial remarks scratched on desks at the end of the class period. Apparently early on in the course, a large group of them had gotten together and made the agreement. It was later revealed to me by one of the more sympathetic students in class, many of the white male students had agreed not to work in my class. It was their belief I would be afraid to fail any white students for fear of parent retaliation! They had agreed to do only those activities or assignments they wanted to and would ignore any they did not want to do. If they didn't want to take a test or quiz they would not do so! They decided that my class would become a study hall to be used for their other classes' assignment.

Determined to solicit participation and involvement in the class, I continued to do a lot of student activities and assignments followed by frequent written assessment. The individual student folders prepared during the pre-school conference days for students' graded assignments were used to file all papers. After reviewing results with the entire class, the day following my grading of the assignments, students were asked to take the papers home for parent signatures. I carefully collected all graded assignments after reviewing with students and filed them in their individual work folder. The majority of these students never brought back the few assignments they were given. I was sending papers home in the other classes, but found the technique could not be used effectively with this class.

A 64% failure rate was calculated for the class at the end of the first grading period. I recorded the large number of failing grades on the appropriate students' report cards, even if it meant putting my job in jeopardy! I was not going to give passing grades for work not done.

Needless to say, when the students received report cards that day, they were shocked and angry. Some class members had their parents call the school to complain.

One can be assured I received a visit from my department chairman the next day. After pulling class folders to show their actual work and revealing the grades in four other classes that were average to good grades, I asked if the school preferred I just give grades? He decided it was the fault of the rebellious group of students and not the teacher. The grades were allowed to stand.

After students and parents were given the reason and, informed the grades would be allowed to stand, there was a renewed effort in class participation the very next day! At the end of the next grading period there was a remarkable turn around in the grades.

It appeared the students had shared this startling experience with their peers in my other classes because there was a renewed effort exerted by some of the previous marginal performing students in my other classes.

Science Office Experiences

After turning in any required reports to the main office, most of my planning period was spent in the Science office each day. There were two rooms to that office. One room had a mimeograph machine (the copier machine of that era) and a typewriter. The other room had a table and chairs to allow a teacher to do work. There were also several shelves of science reference books. My time was always used for its designated purpose of planning. I was usually, making plans for the next day, grading papers or copying materials on the mimeograph machine. At other times, revisits were made to one of the three large stock rooms of supplies to gather equipment for an activity or teacher demonstration.

One of my male colleagues, who saw me frequently browsing in these storage rooms, briefly shared with me a new area of equipment that had been stocked the summer prior to the beginning of the 1966-67-school term. Adding to the wealth of materials and course offerings during that year were numerous pieces of equipment for teaching the concepts of chemistry and physics. This colleague told me, George Washington High School was participating in a test course for a well-known college.

One of the nationally recognized universities, located close by in North Carolina, Duke University had chosen George Washington High School to be among a small group of high schools that would serve as a test site for a new science course. The course was being tested in over 30 different high schools. It was a combination of chemistry and physics taught in a manner that could be understood by high school freshmen. The course dealt with simple laws of physics and basic chemistry.

The title of this class was Quantitative Physical Science (QPS). It was a ninth grade course that basically involved student laboratory activities. Since that was the focus of the class, the college supplied all materials and equipment to teach it. Although the materials were off limits to other teachers during the test years, this large supply of equipment greatly increased the science inventory.

The male colleague had been assigned to teach this experimental course. His room was located next door to the supply room housing the equipment for the course. He delighted in sharing with me the excitement it would bring to our school.

I also found, in talking with him, there was a separate storage room for physics equipment located in our department. Included in this room were our own movie projector and several very good science films I would later use in some of my classes.

Chiseling Walls To Form Entrances

Accepting the Gift but not the Giver

Whether leaving the science office for planning or arriving at school for the day, each time I entered the classroom, I could never let my guard down. Concerted effort was always devoted to maintaining an orderly environment. Being unable to really relax, this naturally created a lot of stress for me.

Gaining classroom control came quicker than anticipated, but gaining acceptance as an individual and their teacher was much slower to occur. It seemed many students accepted the gift, but not the giver. My instructional strategies were accepted, but they were still very much aware of who the teacher was and she was not what they were accustomed to or had learned to accept in this position. I no longer had to deal with noisy disruptive behavior, but there was a different type of ongoing battle to confront...racism, some subtle and other quite overt.

Concerns for Academic Progress

Regardless of the circumstances, academic success for students was at the top of my list of goals and objectives that year. As a custom on my previous job, I tried using the telephone to call a few parents during the very early weeks of the year to discuss their child's progress. This effort did not go very well, however. I quickly realized telephone calls to parents would not be very productive at this point. It became obvious the parents, who had been called, were not ready for discussions with me as a teacher. Some of them were not very pleasant either.

Deciding this would not be a good strategy, at least for a while, I tabled this method of parent contact. A decision was made to send every graded assignment home by students for their parent's signature. The assignments were to be returned the next day and entered in students' individual work folders. I would check off names as I received back the papers and would read out names of any missing papers until they were returned.

Achieving Academic Success

The Strategy

If a way could be found to cut through the thick invisible shield that kept a lot of the students at bay, I knew I could do the required teaching. With the negative attitudes being exhibited, I would not be able to delve directly into teaching as in the past...detours would be required to reach the desired destination. I was still convinced all students were basically the same in being able to learn in the right environment. It became apparent, the classes would need to become an exciting and captivating experience that would generate interest and participation for all students.

Always mindful of the enormous need to maintain control over the learning environment, initially a decision was made to conduct several science demonstrations near the beginning of the period that might be appealing to the students. They would then do written analysis of the results. The demonstrations were done at my large science laboratory desk located in the front of the room. When I saw a need to deviate from a lesson plan to accommodate a particular class with serious student attitudes or learning difficulties, this was always done without hesitation.

Continuing efforts at gaining students' interest, I began to employ other strategies. I had done some public speaking in college and at a few community events prior to coming to Danville. So I began utilizing this expertise at every opportunity in the classroom.

Often, the classes would begin with delivery of a profound statement, a thoughtful quotation or an interesting short story. This was done particularly when introducing new subject matter for study. I quickly observed I could capture the attention of the entire class when using lively and creative verbal approaches to begin a topic. This was usually done as I walked about the classroom while talking.

Unaware, I had a tendency to use hand gestures to create a story telling type of presentation. Students sat attentive during these times.

Being a little artistic proved to be a valuable aid also. At the time, I was able to draw pretty well. This skill had been developed with the numerous drawings and diagrams required to be done in my college science classes. Because of this ability, students sometimes entered the room to find beautiful diagrams or subject matter drawings on the chalkboard. There were also times, while talking, that I would pause to quickly sketch a picture on the board to illustrate a point. The students were amazed.

One of my colleagues, who shared my classroom at a different period, was impressed with a series of diagrams done explaining the process of cell division called mitosis, asked permission to use the drawings during her class.

Another tactic that proved helpful was my ability to write using both hands. In some classes, I would write on the chalkboard with one hand then pick up a piece of chalk with the other hand and continue to write. There were instances in which I would sketch a diagram on the board with my right hand, then label it with a piece of chalk in my left hand. I found later some of the students who thought this to be amazing, had gone home and tried to imitate what I had done.

One of the math teachers would later share with me, he saw one of my students practicing this skill outside of classes; he was so fascinated over seeing this done by his science teacher.

These methods of instruction were continued for a while, as they seemed to work. After gaining their attention in this manner, I began to vary my strategy by introducing other methods of teaching used in my past employment. At least two different strategies were introduced during each class period.

Many lessons plans were developed to include more direct student involvement. Oral presentations by students were assigned on occasions in some of the classes. Having introduced a topic, if there were a need to expand a concept in a different method, I would often assign a student to do an oral presentation on the topic for class credit. A vivid memory of one of these instances was with teaching the operation of the automobile engine. As a part of the physical science curriculum, teachers were required to explain how the car engine worked. In a couple of classes, I assigned this task to two of the male students who were eagerly anticipating enrolling in a driver education course. The science department actually had on loan, a large car engine for demonstration. Some of the teachers chose not to include the engine, but I used it with my classes. A lot of excitement surfaced when I called on the young male students to come to the front of the room and use the model to explain the basic flow of gasoline through the large engine. The visual images were valuable aids in helping students grasp the concept.

A lot of energy was devoted to being a good teacher. I never slacked up during the assigned class periods. Classes always began on time, students were meaningfully engaged, and classes ended on time.

Frequent evaluation of student performance and swift feedback were parts of my lesson plans. After a major test, I would often spend much of the night grading papers to return to the classes the very next day. In many instances this effort would occur after putting the baby to bed for the evening.

Although teaching was not a new field of employment for me, the unusual environment in which it was to occur was definitely new as well as stressful. In this environment, a lot of the people with whom I would need to interact were not openly receptive, students or faculty. When leaving the classroom setting, there were still teachers ignoring me when we came in contact.

Beyond the Classroom

The brief encounter I experienced with the principal as I entered the cafeteria the very first faculty meeting was the only interaction I had with him for several weeks. He never came by my room to my knowledge; there were numerous other responsibilities he had to deal with. His area of work appeared to involve frequent interactions with members of the community and important visitors to the school. There were also various meetings with the superintendent and supervisors from the school board office. He was not very visible in the corridors during the school day, but appeared to remain in the general area of the main office.

There was a little more communication with the assistant principals. The science department chairman, however, did most of the direct and indirect observations of my teaching. Although, the office administration did not spend any time in my classroom, they were very knowledgeable of what was transpiring there, I learned. Students were quickly spreading their experiences throughout the school, especially with the freshmen and sophomore classes. They were also discussing me with the other teachers.

Additional Faculty Meetings

Shortly after the first week of classes, a debriefing type of faculty meeting was held at the end of the school day. Instead of meeting in the cafeteria, again, we met in the school library. This area was very large also. All faculty meetings for the remainder of the year were held in this room.

During that afternoon meeting and subsequent ones, I would occasionally have flashbacks to my first faculty meeting in the school cafeteria and the shock I had experienced. There were many similarities. There were still no other black teachers in the meetings; the scene was basically the same just in a different location.

These faculty meetings were held periodically throughout the year. Some teachers always arrived early and engaged in socializing while waiting for the meeting to begin. I would sometimes arrive early, but was generally not included in the little group talks. Some teachers would speak to me as they entered and others would look away so as to not make eye contact. Just before the meeting began, all teachers would move toward the tables where they generally sat together by departments. This seating pattern facilitated the sharing of information and completion of any needed departmental data during the meetings.

This seating arrangement gave me some degree of comfort because it meant my colleagues from the science department would surround me. The department chairman usually stopped by and spoke before he sat down. All colleagues in the department had an opportunity to converse briefly as we sat together. This helped to ease some of the uncomfortable feeling experienced as the only black teacher in the room.

The principal presided over these meetings and demanded the attention of all present. He was a no nonsense individual who succeeded in keeping everyone focused on the meetings.

While the principal conducted the meetings, one of the assistant principals would quietly circulate throughout the room and take roll of teachers who were present.

Departmental Meetings

All departments held their own meetings throughout the year. Teachers in the science department held their regular meetings in one of the large classrooms on the west wing of the building. Most of the science classes were taught in that area of the building. There would be friendly conversations prior to the beginning of each meeting and I was always included. Among the twelve teachers who made up this department, we taught courses from ninth grade physical science, tenth grade biology, and eleventh grade chemistry up to twelfth grade physics.

An observation was made early in the year that a few male teachers dominated the discussions in these meetings, while a couple of the female teachers had little to say. Initially, any suggestions or comments I offered were never acknowledged. It was as though no one heard me. Then as the discussions continued, one of my colleagues would restate the same idea I had proposed or a very similar one and it would be accepted. That individual would then be given verbal credit for the idea.

I don't even know if the others were aware of these actions, but they were very obvious to me. No one ever made any negative comments to me, however, during these meetings. It was actually the positive encounters I had with members of the science department, during the school day, that helped me get through the many challenging encounters with the students and the faculty at large. I eventually became very close to these teachers in my department.

Three of the teachers continued to stand out in my memory: one male and two females. Both of the female colleagues eventually left the school system and went on to expand their career elsewhere. I experienced a void when they left. The relatively young male colleague, continued to teach until his retirement many years later. Over the years, he proved to be a strong supporter and became a great friend.

Summons To The Principal's Office

Being summoned to the principal's office was something I had always associated with students. There at George Washington high School, however, I found it could also involve teachers.

After the first week of classes, I was called to one of the assistant principal's office to be informed of a parent's complaint. According to his child, a petite female, I had made her sit beside a black student in science class causing her to become very upset. My response was, the intent was to help me learn students by name quickly in order to interact with and help them academically. Assigning students to an alphabetical seating chart helped me learn students quickly so I could refer to them by name, therefore, helping to personalize their education. Skipping around in the alphabetical seating was not a logical method of organizing a class for this purpose. Adjustments would be made at the end of the six weeks grading period, for any student who wanted to be reassigned. By then I would have learned all names. She reluctantly remained in the assigned seat and eventually became friendly with the other student who sat beside her.

I was again called to the assistant principal's office for supposedly missing an afternoon faculty meeting. While it was a practice to have one of the two assistant principals move quietly around the room and take silent attendance, a mistake had occurred. During one meeting, I had inadvertently been overlooked and marked absent. With the intentions of reprimanding me for missing the meeting, I was called to the office by one of the assistant principals.   An apology was offered, however, when I was able to relate to him practically everything that had transpired during the meeting in addition to what he was doing while it took place.

The Summons Kept Coming!

About the fourth week of school, a note was placed in my teacher's mailbox stating the principal would like to meet with me during my planning period. This was definitely a surprise! I was actually going to have an opportunity to sit down and talk with the principal. I was excited! I thought, he wanted to get to know me better as a teacher. Ideas began to pop in my head of things I would eagerly share about myself and my experiences here at the school.

When my planning period began, I headed straight for the office to meet the principal. The main secretary greeted me, and checked to see if he was available. She then walked back to the front desk and directed me to his office.

Shortly after the conference began, I realized this was not a "get to know you better" meeting with the principal! Instead, I was actually being summoned to his office for a reprimand. It appeared a few students from one of my classes had come to him as a group to register a complaint against me. This was that class of male students who consistently tried to challenge my authority as the teacher, but met with stiff opposition from me.   The complaint was I had been informing students of my membership with several black militant groups. The school, he said, would not support that type of behavior from a member of the faculty.

I sat quietly listening. Of all the attempts for students to strike out at me, I thought, this was the most insane one of all. Within my mind, it was obvious the complaint had come from that rebellious class consisting largely of male students.

When he finished, I began talking. I reminded him there were numerous students who would rather I not be assigned as a teacher to the school. Since there were those students who did not want me there, he would constantly have someone come to him with bogus complaints in an effort to have me dismissed. With the obviously precarious situation I found myself in at this large school, I told him, I would hope he considered me intelligent enough not say or do anything to risk creating explosive or resentful reactions. I remember telling him, if it were going to be the position of the administration to oblige students' complaints by continuously summoning me to the office, he could be assured these false reports would not only continue, but they would escalate.

He sat there staring at me and listening to what was being said. When I finished talking, he then cleared his throat in a manner that I would later find to be characteristic of him from faculty meetings, and then told me to go on back to my planning. I was never called to his office again.

Dispelling Myths

I am not sure if one or more of my colleagues were trying to test my honesty, but on several occasions, money was left on the table while I was using the science office alone. I would call the money to the attention of any teacher who entered the room and asked if they had inadvertently left it.

At the beginning of each semester, we were required to assign a small science fee for supplies. I would carefully record names, dates, and amounts collected for each class then give the money to the head biology teacher who was in charge of collecting the fees from teachers. On one occasion, a small group of students broke several glass slides. I collected a small fee from them and turned the money in to the head biology teacher. She seemed surprised one day after I had reported some additional money collected for breakage of equipment and responded that she would never have known if I did not turn the money in to her. No matter how small the sum of money collected for breakage fee, I always reported it.

Another science teacher, a male, who would come in and out of the office on several occasions while I had my planning period, stopped and said to me, "I always heard that black people were lazy, but you are always doing something for your classes or preparing something for future lessons. Most of the teachers use their planning to relax." My actions were definitely being observed and unaware I was helping to dispel some racial myths.

Outside The Classroom

Staff /Faculty Interactions

I continued to eat lunch in the school cafeteria. Each day upon entering the teachers' room I would speak to whomever was seated at my table prior to sitting down with my tray of food. The degree of response varied. Some days, no one responded and on some days, a few brief responses were received. Generally immediately after sitting down, attempts would be made to generate a conversation with the individual directly beside me. In most cases, short responses occurred. Being determined to generate interactions, my behavior routine was repeated daily.

On one occasion, a female teacher asked where I was "from?" It was obvious others were listening to the conversation because when I responded, South Carolina, one of the men at the end of the long table was heard to say to those immediately around him, " I didn't know they even taught them to read down there." I turned in the direction of the comment, laughed and responded, not only do they teach us to read we are taught to read well! Silence filled the room.

The Secretarial Staff

Teachers were required to turn in a variety of reports to the office the first few days of the new school year. The secretarial staff, all of whom were white, received these reports. During my first full planning period, I walked the very long corridor from my room to the main office to turn in a report for attendance and other information. There were several other teachers who apparently had the same planning period as I did and were also turning in their reports.

The main office had five secretaries and one of them was standing behind a long counter, which stretched across the front of the room, to receive materials from teachers. Several teachers handed their material to the secretary and walked out of the office. Finally, as the teacher in front of me handed her report to the receiving secretary, I stepped up to give her my reports. I spoke, handed her my reports and walked out of the office. As I was waking out, I looked back briefly over my shoulders to see her motion for another secretary to come over and they began thumbing through my reports while still standing at the counter. I did not observe this occurring with any of the other reports being turned in. The other reports were simply placed in a stack of papers in a box setting on the counter top.

A similar reaction occurred the very next day as I again turned in a report to the office; only the secretary examined the report alone. These actions were a reminder to me, my entire performance here would be under frequent scrutiny for a while; therefore, I could not do anything haphazardly.

There was one secretary assigned as administrative assistant to the principal. Her job responsibility was carried out in a small office separate from the larger main office. Rarely was she seen out in the main area where teachers and students entered. There was a large glass window through which she could look out into the main office area to monitor the activity that occurred there. Observing her, one could easily see the high degree of professionalism she possessed. She was unmarried and definitely a career woman who took a great deal of pride in her work. She was very knowledgeable of the school and its operations. My interactions with her were infrequent, but pleasant and highly professional. It was she who would call me in for a conference to secure important information for my Federal Income Withholding forms and The Virginia State Retirement System. It was rumored among the faculty that it was she who actually operated the school. She knew all teachers, seniors, and most of the other students by name, I was told.

As the year progressed, it became necessary to make more visits to the main office area where teachers' mailboxes were located or various forms had to be secured. My interaction with the secretaries became more frequent and the relationship became very supportive and friendlier.

Teacher's Lounge

The teachers' lounge was located at the front of the building close to the main office. It was a large rectangular shaped room with a very long table and matching chairs positioned in the middle. Several soft seat chairs were lined up around the walls; with small tables of brochures and educational magazines nearby. A bulletin board at the rear, contained important school notices and announcements. Since there was a sink, vending machines, and restrooms, several teachers used this room to eat lunch or do their planning.

I am not sure how interactions normally occurred in the teacher's lounge. However, during the few times I went during my planning period, interactive with me was nonexistent between the teachers who were present. Since the main office was located close to the teacher's lounge, during my planning after turning in some required reports, I would occasionally go there for a soda from the vending machine. Everyone always seemed pre-occupied with what they were doing, either engaged in a conversation with someone or reading. I would bounce in with a cheery "good afternoon", but received no responses. After purchasing a soda and sitting down to drink it, I noticed no one seemed to acknowledge my presence. It didn't take me long to realize this was an uncomfortable situation I did not have to remain in, so I soon left. I went back to the science office and resumed planning for my classes.

On one occasion, I made an exception and stopped by at the beginning of my lunch period to find the room full of teachers. Many of them were probably choosing to have their lunch in the lounge that day. I had come to the area after turning in some forms to the main office and decided to eat snacks from the vending machines since the cafeteria was so far away from the office.

Entering the teachers' lounge and loudly saying good afternoon, I noticed no one responded. Ignoring the lack of a response, I went directly to the vending machine. Just as I began to put coins in the machine, I heard someone yell out my name from across the room and immediately say I had forgotten to do something very important in homeroom that day. I turned to see who had directed the comment to me. Surprisingly, it was one of my science colleagues, who continued to talk. In the presence of the entire room, she informed me I had neglected to return a form to my homeroom students they were to show their other teachers regarding textbooks. I don't know if she was deliberately trying to embarrass me in the presence of a group or had forgotten where we were at the time.

Rather than exhibit anger, I casually responded, " With the large group of tasks teachers were required to complete in homeroom this morning, forgetting to return those slips was probably not the only thing I had forgotten to do". Someone actually snickered.

Keeping my reaction in check, I put the food items in my purse and left the lounge. Eating in the science office, I thought would be a better choice that day.

The colleague later came to me and apologized. She said she wasn't thinking, when she spoke to me in the lounge the way she had. According to her explanation, she had planned to inform me of the oversight I had made in homeroom. Seeing me in the lounge triggered her memory. I then reminded her the students had already presented the forms to their other teachers several days that week. My forgetting to re-issue them that day should not have been a major problem.

Beyond The School's Reach

When the last bell rang for the day-that was the end of my associations with the staff. It was like moving into a different environment with many new players and entirely different rules. Accidental encounters with colleagues out in the community, would result in the colleague appearing not to want it known to their associates they knew me.

During the weekends, occasionally I would see one of the staff or faculty member out in the city at the grocery store or one of the department stores. I would wave or if close enough, I would say hello. It soon became pretty obvious in this different setting the rules had changed and they were not favorable to integration. The individual would turn to look in a different direction or would walk to another area of the facility to avoid having to meet me face to face. There were instances, I would see a faculty member who shared the same lunch schedule and talked to me during the period. I would smile and walk towards the teacher, who was apparently with family members or friends, to say hello. Just as I approached they would abruptly turn and walk away.

It was a little painful, but I realized the city still had some major obstacles to overcome before the idea of true integration would occur. I had to remind myself, the school system's experiment with me being assigned to GWHS was still in its infancy stages also.

There were a few instances in which I saw students out in the community. These sightings were usually during the weekends at a shopping center or a large department store. I would wave, if the student was one with whom I had developed a good working relationship in class. It was surprising to observe, however, the students like the teachers, would look away to keep from acknowledging me. One young lady was with her parents and told me the next day; she could not speak to me in public because her father would disapprove.

Teachers' Professional Association

A very painful incident occurred early in the year when I attended an after school meeting of the Danville Education Association (DEA). This was a teachers' professional organization consisting of teachers across the entire school system. The meeting was held in the auditorium of George Washington High School because of its ability to accommodate a very large group of individuals. The faculty had received an announcement asking all teachers to attend this first meeting of the New Year. Three teachers had stopped by my room and invited me to accompany them to the meeting and we would sit together. It was usually not very long they assured me.

What I didn't know at the time was the meeting was for all white teachers in the school system. Shortly after the meeting began one of the organizers on the stage made the statement there were uninvited persons present. The meeting he said was only for members. There was a lot of mumbling among the individuals present and heads turned in my direction. I just sat there; I was not about to get up and walk out of the room. One brave male stood up from the floor and stated, "No one is a member yet because we are beginning a new year and no memberships have been secured for this year." There was a quietness that occurred over the audience.

The presider then continued the meeting, discussing the goals of the organization and soliciting memberships. It was a short meeting, but not because of the incident. I later learned there were two separate teachers associations in the city, one white Danville Education Association (DEA) for all teachers who taught in white schools and one black, Danville Teachers Association (DTA) for all teachers who taught in a black school. In my unique position, I was apparently caught in the middle of this arrangement. The teachers with whom I sat apologized as we left the meeting, although they had done nothing wrong. After leaving the meeting, I headed straight to my car.

Parental Interactions

Open House

My first direct contact with parents came during an Open House held one evening for parents. At that time the school did not have a Parent- Teachers Association (PTA) affiliated with it. This event was considered to be the major contact medium for large groups of parents to interact with their child's teachers.

By the time the first open house event was scheduled, I had already started to make some progress in interactions with many of my students. Several parents probably came that evening out of curiosity rather than concern for their child's progress in class. There were many whose goal may have been to see this African American teacher. The number of parents who came by my room was impressive compared to what I had sometimes experienced at my previous job.

In preparing for the meeting, I had taken great care to organize all students' folders, alphabetically and display them on two long student laboratory tables located on one side of the room. The tables were close to my desk, which permitted easy access and allowed me to keep an eye on them.

The first group of parents that came by the room took me

by surprise as they immediately sat down instead of coming up to the desk individually and speaking with me. Realizing they were probably expecting a general presentation, I used the opportunity to provide the entire group with an overview of the courses, the school's requirement and my expectations. It was during this brief presentation that I was able to explain the use of the individual student folders and students performance records. Parents were invited to find their child's folder to review their work and come up individually to confer with me, if they chose to do so. The folders had been arranged by class periods, then alphabetically by students' last names.

Some parents were very pleasant as they talked with me that evening. A few just spoke after viewing their child's folders, then left the room. I couldn't help, but notice there were also those who chose not to say anything to me as they entered or exited the room. That group simply browsed the contents of their child's folder then left the room.

I vividly recall one unpleasant conference with a couple that evening. The parents (a husband and wife) entered my room after all of the others had left and began scolding me for their child's failing grades in my class. The child, a male student, had received some failing grades in my class and the parents were upset with me, not their son. Neither parent addressed me by name, as they approached my desk. The father just verbally tore into me with his complaint, instead.

To set the tone, for a civil conversation, I remember asking " and you are of the parent of which student?" The mother appeared a little embarrassed when she realized they had used an inappropriate approach. The father, who appeared to be a prominent figure in the community, shared with me, in an angry tone of voice, that he and his wife had promised their son a big trip to Florida if he received passing grades in all his classes. According to the father, because of failing grades in my class they would not be able to give their son the trip. They wanted me to change his grades.

Both parents were asked to accompany me to the table of student work folders and we would pull the one for their son. Picking up the folder then handing it to the father, both parents were asked to sit down with me at a vacant table so we could view their son's work together. While holding the son's folder in his hand, he flipped through the contents. Handing the folder back to me, he said in his opinion, the few papers he saw weren't sufficient to determine a course grade.

Re-opening the folder, the parents were asked to carefully observe the grades on those few assignment; they represented very poor quality of class work. Additionally, I revealed that there were several missing assignments he had neglected to do. The son consistently failed to turn in assignments or make up several missed quizzes and tests. There should have been about twelve graded papers in the folder up to this point and their son only had five. They were D's and one F.

Sensing these parents needed convincing, I walked over to the table and randomly picked up three other student folders. Swiftly flipping through the folders so as not to reveal names, both parents could see the other folders were full of graded assignments and most had good grades.

Their son had failed to complete graded work and would not consent to make up any assignments missed due to absences. The science department held a joint makeup session one day a week, after school to allow students an opportunity to make up any assignments missed due to approved absences. Students who had assignments to make up were reminded with a list placed on the board.

The father's position was the missing assignments should just be disregarded. I had to assure him this was not the position of our school or any school in determining students' grades. Exceptions could not be made for their son who had apparently been irresponsible. Not being able to convince the father his son had not done the work required to earn higher grades, he began to criticize me. According to the son, the teacher did not speak clearly so he had difficulty understanding her. I found the comment to be amusing since no one had ever made that accusation before.

It was disheartening to see, the father still refused to accept the fact his son was behaving irresponsibly regarding his class work. In spite of what was revealed in the class folder, he wanted the missing assignments ignored and the son graded on the few pieces of work he had done.

Turning his anger toward me, he said my class would be the only one preventing them from providing the trip to Florida as had been promised. Looking at the wife, her facial expressions hinted she fully understood it was her son's fault, but was afraid to speak out against the husband. They were assured I would be happy to work with the son, in the future, to help make up any missed assignments.

Both were encouraged to keep a daily check on the son's assignments in all classes and call me periodically, to check his progress. As I began to thank them for coming to the Open House, the father tossed the folder on my desk and huffed out of the room.

The next day, I immediately checked the office records and found the son was failing in three of his subjects. Unfairly, the parents had attempted to target me as the only teacher in whose class their son was performing unsatisfactory.

Several weeks into the semester, an unexpected parent

conference occurred at the end of a regular school day. Surprisingly, a parent showed up one afternoon for an unscheduled conference. It was immediately after school had ended. My last student had just left the room when I looked up to see a strange gentleman enter through the door. Walking toward my desk, he immediately introduced himself as the father of one of my male students. As he began to speak, it became obvious that he was there to try and persuade me to change a grade for his son who was an athlete. He wanted to be assured that his son would be eligible to participate in a particular sport the next semester. In order to participate, he would need good grades in all classes.

The son was currently earning very poor grades in my science class. In working closely with various students, while the entire class was involved in individual assignments, the son had informed me that science had always been a very difficult subject for him. The father was probably already aware of that fact. He was assured I would be happy to stay after school to provide extra help for his son, but could not give grades to any students. Realizing he would not be able to persuade me to change or give grades, he left the room in an angry mood.

What was not known at the time was, the parent had not reported to the office first; something he was required to do. Instead, he had come directly to my classroom to try and influence my decision. His intent may have been to try and intimidate me into changing grades.

The Stress Continued

As the semester continued, teaching at this school had become very stressful! A lot of students were receptive of my teaching, but seemingly not receptive of me. There were still students in homeroom who were not interacting with me. Although racial remarks were not being slung at me, attitudes definitely revealed a dislike for my position as a teacher. Some students were not only failing to warm up to my presence, but were deliberately avoiding any close contact with me. This was shown through the failure to acknowledge my presence even when passing by me standing at the door of the entrance to the room.

The academic workload was unreal! I taught five classes daily, averaging about thirty students per class, which gave me a master roll of about 150 students that first semester. Teaching this number of classes translated into at least 2 sets of 150 papers to grade per week. Desiring to make a fair assessment of the students' academic progress I was assigning tests or quizzes and grading science laboratory exercises weekly. The grading was mainly done after school hours because only a limited number of papers could be graded within the fifty minutes of planning provided.

During the administration of semester exams, it seemed teachers were almost expected to be magicians. If two exams were assigned per day, the grading was required to be done outside the school day. In addition to checking the large number of papers, grades needed to be computed for each student and report cards completed. The exams and report cards for those classes were required in the main office upon arriving at school the next morning. This information was needed by the guidance department to make adjustments to the scheduling of classes for the new semester.

While the exams were actually being administered, teachers were required to frequently walk around the room and monitor the process. No grading of papers, planning, or other teacher distractions were to occur during the administering of the exams.

So, after working several hours on the job during the day, it was often necessary to continue some work at home, especially during examination time. Additionally, as the first semester came to an end lesson plans needed to be developed for the new classes assigned to be taught.

The semester concept was indeed new to me with all of the unusual demands placed on the classroom teacher. This arrangement for the delivery of instruction seemed equivalent to having two different years crammed within the span of nine months. Pressure was felt more severely by a teacher just entering the school than one who had spent at least a year there. As a teacher's tenure increased, it became easier to accumulate and recycle many of their lesson plans reducing the pressure of preparing for new classes.

*"At times, I felt I had
the weight of the entire black race
on my shoulders"*

With the many tough challenges being faced daily, it seemed I was constantly engaged in an uphill battle. Progress was being made in some areas while it appeared to elude me in others. Teaching was dear to me and although I never dwelled on race, having been put in this unusual test case was a whole different ball game that went beyond regular teaching.

There were times I felt I had the weight of the entire black race on my shoulders. So much was riding on my ability to succeed in this environment.

Flashbacks to my early teen years began occurring. I kept getting the feeling of being prepared for something special in my future; something that would require a lot of strength and courage. I didn't know what it would be or when it would occur, but the feeling kept surfacing.

It slowly became clearer ... the whole situation was not about me, but encompassed something much bigger that extended far beyond me as an individual. It was about me being used as an instrument to aid in a greater cause.

If I failed at this initial effort of the school system to integrate the faculty, it could seriously affect the process of adding other black teachers into this setting. Fate, it seemed, had issued me the challenge of helping to pave the way for others to come. During many of my reflective and thought-provoking moments, I faced the startling realization that in this situation and at this important moment in time, "*failure was not an option.*" If I failed this crucial test it could seriously impede the progress of school integration in Danville. No way could I allow this to occur! I was cautiously walking an educational tightrope and couldn't afford to be toppled over by forces eagerly wishing for that to occur.

In the back of my mind remained the awareness that

Danville was a highly segregated city at the time and what I was doing had never been done here before. However, I was determined, to succeed no matter how huge the challenge! My efforts intensified as I developed an unrelenting determination to succeed in spite of the sometimes-harsh environment.

Varied Teaching Techniques

Renewing my determination, I continued to vary teaching techniques by introducing many of those strategies proven to be effective in the past. Once implemented, those efforts appeared to heighten the learning process and elicited more student participation. They seemed to keep students engaged in the learning process while directing attention away from the teacher. My goal was to utilize at least two different strategies during most class periods. The major exception was during test time. We were doing a lot of "hands-on" activities well before the concept became so popular in later years.

During class periods when it became necessary to use lecture as a method of instruction, we would follow-up with an activity engaging the entire class that would serve as reinforcement to the lesson's objectives.

To provide continuity in the learning process, I would summarize the previous day's lesson prior to beginning each new day's assignment. At the end of each class, a brief review or summary of the lesson we had just completed would be provided. At times, students would be asked to do the summarizing. Many seemed to enjoy this activity, as student volunteers in each class were involved.

When developing tests, if the format was to include True/False questions they would be designed differently. A correct answer would require more than a mere guess. With each true/false statement, a word would be underlined that would make the statement true or false. If the statement was false, students were required to write, in the blank space beneath the statement, a term that would make the statement true. Both parts of the statement had to be correct in order to receive credit for a correct answer.

Furthering a determination to offer variety in teaching methods, my attention was sometimes directed beyond the storage rooms and the regular classroom.

Visits were made to the library a few times during my planning period to introduce myself to the library staff. The head librarian was a female whose name was Dolly. The first encounter was awkward. I followed this visit with a few additional ones. Each time I would ask for the location of an item until the staff became more receptive of me. After the library personnel became more cordial, a discussion was initiated around the possibility of bringing science classes to the library for research. They were receptive to the possibility and amazed to find I was interested in using their facility in this manner.

Continuing to enhance the learning process in class, students were assigned small group investigations, periodic library research, and oral presentations. There were times I would take an entire class to the library in order to provide an " even" playing field for those who lacked access to reference books and materials at home.

It was after the first grading period ended that I actually took the first of my classes to the library. Behavior expectations were reviewed, prior to leaving the classroom. Clear instructions were given regarding the assignment and how they would proceed with the research once we arrived at the library. Upon entering the library, we were met by the librarian, Dolly, who directed us to a seating area she had reserved for the class. Students were allowed to move around the room as they began to research their topics. A few, I noticed, approached the library staff for needed assistance, which they eagerly provided. The students were actively engaged the entire period. There was no loud talking or any playing around.

When we left, the librarian commended me for the wonderful behavior of the students and invited us back for additional days of research.

Frequent visits to the science supply rooms became a standard part of my planning period. Initially, when some laboratory equipment was desired to reinforce the concepts of a particular lesson, I would draft a list, include the date needed and give it to my department chairman. He would collect the items and bring them to my room at the beginning of the designated period. After a few of these requests, he assured me it was okay to secure the materials on my own. With this approval, I would frequently load up my portable cart with various pieces of equipment that were not been used by any of the other teachers and take this to my classrooms. It wasn't long before I knew basically every piece of equipment and teaching aid owned by the department and the location.

Several of the other teachers were favoring a lecture method with occasional laboratory activities for their classes. I was excited over the large inventory of equipment and was eager to put it to good use.

It was interesting to observe the amount of enthusiasm generated in the various classes with the use of test tubes, glass beakers and balances. These pieces of equipment always seem to aid in eliciting full class participation.

When away from the classroom, efforts were constantly being made to smooth the transitional phase into the larger school family.

Each day, a trip would be made to the cafeteria for lunch. Attempts were made to either initiate conversations or join others that were centered on some school topic. It was slow going, but some of the teachers who ate regularly in the cafeteria became more tolerant of me and would speak. I tried staying longer periods in their midst rather then just eating and leaving. Some teachers became more approachable. They would sit down and immediately speak or ask how was my day. There were a few, however, who let it be known, through body language, that they were not interested in any interactions.

As the semester progressed, when passing teachers in the corridors, some would actually stop for a brief conversation. The first time that happened, there were three teachers walking together who met me in the corridor during one of my trips to the main office to turn in reports. As they approached each spoke and one even asked, " How was your day?" I looked back to see if the remarks were being directed to someone behind me and found there was no one there. It was a good feeling, as I smiled to myself.

I was beginning to make more progress with the students. After several tense weeks, it became apparent their dislike for me was being overtaken by appreciation of the abundance of aid I was providing in this huge frightening new school. This does not mean all students began to like me, but their actions became more like those of regular students toward a regular teacher.

It was during the school's celebration of the Christmas holidays, that I experienced examples of more positive responses from my homeroom students indicating an easing of the racial barrier. The Student Cooperative Association (SCA) had planned an activity for all homerooms that would become an in-school contest. Classes were asked to decorate the outside door to their homeroom with a Christmas scene. The doors would be judged to determine the best and most creative. It was surprising that my homeroom representatives to the SCA came to me very excitedly and asked if we (our class) could participate. They also asked if I would be willing to allow them an opportunity to plan the activity and decorate during homeroom period.

Students either donated money or brought items from home to use. We didn't win, but I observed a lot of excitement in the planning and decorating. Some students would come up to me and ask for my opinion on certain ideas they had regarding the decorations.

On the day the Christmas vacation was to begin, all students were allowed to return to their homerooms for a brief celebration during the last period of the day. Earlier in the week, the entire student body had been allowed to order holiday desserts from one of the school's clubs to eat during this time.

Most of my homeroom students did not bother to order any of the food that was being sold as a fundraiser for one of the school clubs. However, upon returning to homeroom that afternoon, to their surprise, each one received something to eat.

Many of the students were never aware, but I had purchased a small bag of treats for each of them to be eaten during this time. Since this was their first celebration at GWHS, most left for the holidays thinking the school had provided these for everyone. I never mentioned the bags had actually come from me. The important thing was it brought smiles to their faces, which was something I had not seen often. In the spirit of the holiday season it was my desire to add to their excitement.

When the class returned after the winter vacation, two of the female students told me their friends did not receive food in their homeroom on the day of the Christmas vacation; I smiled. These two students, Pamela and Laurie then realized I had been the one to provide the treats for our homeroom class.

It had been during the same week leading up to the Christmas holidays, I recall attending my first school assembly program with the entire student body in attendance. All 2,300 students and the entire faculty attended. This large event was held in the school gymnasium. I was happy my classroom was located on the same hallway a short distance from the gym. This meant I did not have to become engulfed in the massive flow of students headed toward this one room.

Boxes of canned goods and other items collected in homerooms were taken to this assembly where they were to be distributed to a selected charitable institution. The recipient for that year was The Faith Home for Children. These items had been collected during the same time students were busy decorating homeroom doors for the judging contest.

After seating my class on two rows of bleachers, I looked over the mass of students assembled. It was amazing to see that many students together in one school. They came in noisy, but quieted down to hear the thank you remarks from the SCA representatives. Scanning the room, I saw very few African American students scattered throughout this huge group of students assembled.

With the large number of students enrolled, rarely did the

opportunity present itself for me to come in direct contact with the African American students not assigned to my classes. There was one young attractive female student who stands out in my memory. Usually the only time I saw her was periodically during the changing of classes and usually from a distance. She always walked very close to the wall as she moved swiftly to her next class. I never got an opportunity to pull her aside and share her experiences. She was always observed walking alone in the corridors and I never saw her interact with her peers. The corridors were always full of students during the changing of classes.

This young lady, who appeared to be a junior or senior, was probably one of the few students who had broken the racial barrier earlier. With the exception of a couple of male students who were good athletes, the other few African American students appeared to exist in a maze of invisibility.

Confrontation With The Department Chairman

Things were moving in the right direction, I began thinking. Then, as the first semester was nearing an end, I walked into the science department office one day to find the department chairman, who was responsible for assigning classes for all science teachers each semester, in conference with one of the other teachers. As I entered, he looked up to see me, and then mentioned he would need to talk with me about second semester classes after completing his conference with the teacher already engaged in discussion. Continuing, he stated he had already spoken with each of the other teachers; there were ten others. Matter-of- factly, he stated I would have to take what was left and named the classes. Listening to the list, I realized they were all very slow academic classes with the potential for creating a lot of discipline problems.

I was hurt, not only over being the last one contacted, but also over the prospect of the many problems that would be added to the challenging school experiences already being encountered. Before I thought, the words slipped out, " No I will not"! Looking up at me in shock, he sat there for a few moments as the teacher in conference also registered a look of disbelief. He was caught off guard with my response. I followed up the first response with: " I will not accept that terrible assignment and beside, I don't appreciate being last! I'll resign first, then go tell the superintendent why I resigned."

After pausing for a few minutes he finally said we would discuss the situation later. The fact that what I thought had actually translated into spoken words took me by surprise too. As it turned out, I was assigned a different schedule.

I often thought at the end of that first semester, Wow! Will the challenges here ever end?

Although I did not meet my department chairman during the first few preschool conference days, I found him to be very supportive and we became good friends as the year progressed. I think the brief disagreement in the science office over my class schedule was a healthy exchange. It helped us to really begin to see and accept each other as just another teacher rather than as a black and white teacher. Near the end of that year, he laughed and told me I sure had a lot of spunk to be in my situation!

The Beginning of Acceptance

As the semester progressed, word was spreading that my classes were interesting and different. Students began telling their peers to try and get Mrs. Fullerwinder for physical science or biology next semester.

One of my colleagues, said some students asked him who is Fullerwinder? "We heard she was a good teacher." They were surprised when he pointed me out to them. None of the students realized, with a name like Fullerwinder, I was a black teacher.

According to the guidance department, a few students actually altered their written schedules and assigned themselves to my class. Of course, when this illegal act was caught, those students were pulled from my class rolls and given the correct assignment. I ended up with one class for a couple of days; so large I couldn't see the desks from the front of the room. It was chaotic until the schedules were readjusted.

A teacher in the foreign language department came up to me in the corridor, one afternoon, at the end of a stressful day, and said, she could relate to what I must be experiencing because she was the first teacher of Jewish descent to join this faculty. She had succeeded in gaining acceptance over the years and eventually became a department chairman. She praised me for being able to keep my classes under control in this unusual situation. The students, she said, were spreading the word that I was pretty strict and she smiled.

Walking down the central hall between classes one day near the middle of the first semester, I heard from a distance, a male student say to the group of male students with whom he was walking, " Hey! There's a "n" lady in the halls". They responded, "where?" As I glanced toward their direction…one student in the group said, "Oh, that's just Mrs. Fullerwinder, my science teacher, come on lets go". With that response, all turned and continued on to their classes.

Other students who knew me were now passing me in the corridors and speaking; actually addressing me by name.

My department chairman, apparently feeling comfortable enough with my level of proficiency, asked me to assist him in computing the percentage of students passing and failing in each course taught in the science department. The percentages would include all classes of the twelve teachers of science. This very important report was required by the main office and had to be accurate. I was not a random choice since he had come to my classroom earlier to make the request.

One day, shortly before lunch was to begin, I snagged my stocking on a classroom chair. Mentioning this incident to one of my female colleagues, Joy, who taught in my room the next period, she offered me a pair of hers. Since this was before the days of varied colored stockings for women, her very light colored stockings would have attracted more attention than the ruin in my dark colored ones. The admirable thing was her response demonstrated that she was not thinking of me as a black teacher, but rather as just another female teacher. She had responded the way she would have responded to another white teacher.

Apparently the successes experienced with students were aids to gaining more acceptances from the staff. The students had begun discussing my classes in the presence of other teachers and many complimentary things were said. When entering my room, I had observed, several students were now greeting me by name.

The beginning of acceptance, as an individual, and not as a black teacher was beginning to occur.

As The Semester Ended

After my first encounter with having to grade a mountain of exams, it seemed, the semester came to an end. Close to five months had been spent at this very large institution and the first semester was finally over! All of this happened near the end of January 1967.

By the time the first semester ended, I was literally exhausted from trying to develop interesting, intriguing, and student engaged lesson plans. During the previous five months, I must have introduced students to every piece of science related equipment in the school. They had done investigations and laboratory exercises to enhance scientific concepts. We had made trips to the library for research, engaged in small group work and listened to individual presentations. During the presentations, I observed several students who chose to deliver their oral reports in a competitive mode with each other. The efforts produced a good learning environment.

It had indeed been a trying semester and I was glad when it was finally behind me! Although most learned a good deal of science, it would have been very difficult to survive more than one semester like that one.

Reflecting over the semester, and the many headache-generating experiences, no one had openly called me a derogatory name (although some had been written) and no one had ever attempted to strike me!

Did I win them all over, students and teachers? No! but it was obvious I had begun to earn a lot more tolerance… maybe even acceptance!!

On The Home Front

With the first semester coming to an end, I had an opportunity to reflect and remember significant events that had occurred. Not only did that reflective period enable me to highlight school events, it also offered a reminder of the tremendous support I had received at home.

Whereas I was not always getting the emotional support from the faculty as a whole, I was fortunate to have a loving and supportive husband at home. If I came home and seemed to have had an usually stressful day, John would carry the family out for our evening meal or even cook, himself. He was always willing to lend a listening ear to my concerns or frustrations.

It was interesting to note that he, too, had been assigned, that year, as the first black teacher to Mt. Herman Elementary School located just a few miles away in Pittsylvania County. Having taught previously at the all black Central Elementary School he had been transferred to Mt. Hermon Elementary the same year that I went to George Washington High School. Although assigned to teach much younger students who as a whole were more accepting…he had his share of challenges in trying to gain the approval of parents and some of the teachers.

John provided tremendous support during the crucial

period of administering examinations to my classes, at the end of the semesters. After we put the baby to bed, he would help with stapling together all of those papers. We would spread out the papers on our living room floor as we worked as a team to collate and staple together sets of papers for my five different classes. The office machines were not able to collate the papers so this had to be done manually. With 150 sets of exam papers spread out on the floor, often we couldn't see the carpet beneath.

While stapling papers, we would often reminiscence over my short time in Danville. I had stayed in South Carolina teaching after our marriage, and had only come to Danville just after our first child, Arthur Lamont, was born. Near the end of the year, I had become very lonely in this new town. So with John's approval, I called the principal at Langston High, the black high school, to ask if I could substitute a few days in order to get out of the house some.

The principal, an elderly black female, was very nice and invited me in to do just that. I found a very reliable individual whose sister had attended college with my husband to keep the baby and allow me the brief experience of substitute teaching a couple of times. Over the years, this young lady and her family, the Ingrams, became strong supporters and friends to us.

Our son, Arthur, was going to turn a year old by the end of the summer and before the next school term, so I had decided to apply for a full time teaching position in the school system. Little did I know that I would be hired for George Washington High School.

Beginning The Half-Way Mark

Second Semester

After completing the hectic period of final examinations, grades were averaged, report cards were prepared and adjustments were made to class schedules. Students were given a two- day semester break, which allowed teachers an opportunity to complete this change process. The second semester then began with students first reporting back to their homerooms to secure report cards and new class schedules.

For me, the new semester brought all new classes and largely new students. It was literally, the half- way mark for the year. I was a little excited because the new semester had given me an opportunity to say goodbye to that very challenging class that consisted mainly of young men, many who had never really accepted me.

Starting over with a different group of students, as it was soon revealed, was not necessarily a wonderful thing. After having successfully learned all my students by name with the aid of seating charts, I was then assigned a new set of students for the second semester. This meant having a new group of 150 students to learn, interact with and teach. The additional numbers produced a total of approximately 330 students for the school year, including the homeroom group. I had taken on a personal challenge to learn every student in my classes by name and actually succeeded in doing so.

As the second semester began, I had to introduce myself to a new group of students. A pleasant contrast to the previous semester was in the way students would enter my classroom. Most of the students spoke as they entered and then took their seats. Many of them had heard of me, so were aware of the class expectations, and were willing to stay in my classes.

Slowly, some of the same attitudes encountered during the beginning of the first semester resurfaced among this group, but thank goodness they were not in the majority. There were students, some males in particular, who refused to address me by name. They would simply blurt out what they wanted me to know. Each time, I would remind them of the proper procedures for addressing a teacher.

My assigned lunch period also changed which meant having to encounter a different group of teachers when eating in the cafeteria. Effort was again required to try and blend in as attempts were made to generate conversations with a mostly new group of staff members. For some of these teachers, I had not had an opportunity for close up contact. There were also those who had only been seen from a distance during the after school faculty meetings.

Although having to adjust to a different group of lunch associates, it was a relief over the first semester. Flashbacks to first semester, reminded me, it was then I had to be introduced to an entire school faculty! It was during the past semester, all teachers had to adjust to the idea that a black teacher had dared to invade their space and become a part of the staff.

Shortly into the second semester, I could feel a difference in the atmosphere. An air of progression was sensed when I first entered the room. Some teachers would initiate conversations at the table. Others would speak as they sat down with food trays. Even with the progress, I still encountered a few teachers who chose to ignore my presence.

As biology classes were added to my schedule that semester there were many interesting experiences encountered.

Some of my classes were taught on the west wing of the building in Room W105. Although it was great for laboratory investigations, the room's design presented its own share of challenges. There were seven long laboratory tables around the room that served as student desks. These seven tables were to accommodate twenty-eight to thirty students during a class period. There were four to six students seated together. Distractions could easily occur. It required me to be extremely attentive.

The laboratory experience on blood typing, mentioned earlier, actually occurred during that semester. It was just one of many very interesting eye-opener observations during the first year.

Another experience that remains fresh in my memory also occurred in one of my biology laboratory classes. I had just finished a class demonstration at my desk for the entire class to observe. Upon completing the activity, I washed my hands in the sink connected to the teacher's desk and reached for a paper towel. I was still talking to the class summing up the results of the activity they had just observed, but noticed the students were focused on the paper tower being used to dry my hands. Continuing to slowly dry my hands and then toss the towel into the trashcan, I noticed all eyes were fixed on the towel as it was dropped into the trashcan. It then occurred to me they were watching to see if any of the color from my hands had rubbed off on the paper towel. Chuckling to myself, the thought occurred, this is another example of dispelling a myth. The color on dark skin as with any skin is colorfast and does not rub off.

Since the students would be engaged in several small group investigations and laboratory work in the biology classes, groupings were assigned at the beginning of the semester. Two students were usually assigned to a group. After the first activity that involved the dissection of small animals, a few revisions were made in the groups.

I had observed that some of the females in the same group appeared very squeamish about touching some of the preserved specimens, so I reassigned them to a different partner. It was particularly obvious when a laboratory activity involved dissecting a frog. A few of the girls refused to touch the animals. When I saw a sincere look of fear on their faces, rather than risk them fail the class, some adjustments were made in the assignments. A strong student was paired with one who found it different to actually handle the lab materials.

A few weeks into the second semester, a transfer student from outside our school district was added to my biology class roll. This was a white male, who obviously did not know he was being assigned to a black teacher. When entering the room, he frowned and looked down at the schedule held in his hand. Looking up, he then asked if this was Mrs. Fullerwinder's class? When I responded that I was Mrs. Fullerwinder, his face turned very red. A name like Fullerwinder had apparently made him assume the teacher was white. At first, he hesitated then slowly walked toward my desk and extended his schedule.

After recording his name on my roll, I extended a

welcome, and then invited him to participate in an ongoing class activity. He was directed to a seat and a small group of students with whom he could work.

Slowly, he walked across the room and sat down, then immediately placed his head on his desk. I chose not to create a scene, but after observing his reaction, was determined to succeed at getting participation from him in class.

The class was involved in a laboratory investigation using the compound microscopes. Observing him and the disinterest shown, I decided to add some extra excitement to the activity. The students were observing prepared slides, but I went to the storage room to retrieve a small jar of pond water, intended for another day. The water was teeming with harmless live, very mobile microorganisms similar to the ones on their prepared slides. I walked around the room and placed a drop of water on the slide of each group.

Shortly after observing the slides under their microscope, some of the girls started squealing with excitement and began encouraging their classmates to come and look at the slide. With the first squeal, the young man sat up and looked around, but remained seated. He then slowly returned his head to his desk.

Pretty soon, half the class, was displaying excitement, and inviting each other over to the different stations to witness the movement of the weird organisms moving about on the various glass slides. After, several comments and students eagerly moving from one microscope to another, squealing, the young man sat up. He then walked over to one of the student stations near him and asked to look through their microscope. After observing, for a few minutes, the activity occurring through the microscope, I was surprised when he turned and came up to my desk. Not referring to me by name, he asked for a microscope and the "stuff" students were observing. Although he had failed to address me by name, I wasn't very concerned because I had won a much greater battle; I had won his interest and desire to participate in class that day.

A New Class Experience...Supervised Study Hall

In order to accommodate six periods of class offerings for the large student body, some students were assigned one period of in-school study. This class was generally held in one of the large rooms on the east end of the building where rehearsals for plays often occurred after school hours. Listening to conversations of students while involved in small group activity, I learned some of these periods were chaotic. It was not uncommon to have a few students report to the room with no materials for study then spend the time talking with their peers. Some would engage in loud conversations across the room, making it difficult for others to concentrate in the noisy environment.

Some of the teachers, who did not like this responsibility added to their schedules, were not as consistent in maintaining order. Small group of students were allowed to attend the library during this assigned period.

During the second semester, I was assigned as a supervisor over one of these study hall sessions. This group being extremely large was assigned to the cafeteria with two teachers as supervisors. It was interesting to find my co-supervisor for the session was the same male coach who had stood outside my classroom door that very first day of classes. He was well respected by the students, but a no-nonsense individual who believed study halls were designed for study.

The coach's presence in the room helped me to gain the acceptance of students. Initially, it was he who established guidelines to be adhered to in the class. On the first day, he immediately spread the students out over the cafeteria so that an empty seat would be located between each person. No one was ever permitted to enter the room without study materials. The room was quiet and conducive to study. The two of us would alternate checking roll and providing any additional instructions when necessary.

After a few weeks, there would be days he did not report to the session leaving me alone to supervise the group.

There were instances in which he needed extra time to prepare for a football game scheduled that evening and used the period to handle important athletic tasks. The students continued to behave well for me when he was not present. Other teachers would enter the cafeteria with a surprised look, when he was away, and comment on how unbelievable it was the students were actually quiet and studying.

In the Regular Classrooms

Back in my regular classes, there were a few students who were finding science classes to be very challenging. When assigning individualized work, I would try to provide extra assistance to those students. This practice proved itself to be very helpful with some of the students. About mid-way through the first grading period, I was able to encourage a young man to continue working on an assignment until he succeeded. After introducing the topics of Fahrenheit and Centigrade temperatures, students were assigned problems, which included converting these readings from one to the other. As I circulated around the room, this young man was observed to be just sitting there not working. When asked why, he responded that he couldn't do the problems. I verbally encouraged him to try, but he insisted he could not work the problems.

With a little gentle persuasion, I remember asking him to let me see that he could not do the problem. He looked up at me and stated that he didn't know how to begin. When I told him to first write the problem, then try to remember the rule. He did as I asked, but after copying the problem down on paper, again repeated that he couldn't do them. Again, I insisted that he let me see him try. It was obvious that he was becoming a little angry with me as he picked up his pencil and began to write.

The exciting thing, however, is once he actually starting working at the problem, he found he got the correct answer. This led to a continuation of work on the remainder of the assignment. We both felt good about his success. Before leaving his desk, I whispered, " you can't succeed until you first try." He smiled as he continued to work.

Later, one of the assistant principals stopped me as I entered the main office area and invited me into his office for a few minutes to just talk. He asked how things were going in my various classes. During the conversation, I was able to share this experience along with some other positive experiences. This, I thought was a good example to share of student performance.

There continued to be more good experiences during the second semester as compared to the one that had just ended. Although things were moving in a better direction, out of nowhere, I could expect the unexpected to surface. It became a wise course of action to always remain alert.

There were occasions on which non-instructional factors

would surface to create periods of stress. One unexpected and frustrating experience occurred when a fire drill was held by the school administration. While teaching in one of the rooms to which I was assigned on the west wing the fire alarm sounded. Recognizing this sound, I immediately grabbed my roll book and purse as I directed the students to an exit at a back door designated for that room. There was a door to the room that emptied into a very small area with another door that led to the outside of the building. Once outside the building, the class lined up and I checked the roll to make sure everyone was accounted for. There were other classes lined up in the same general area. After a brief period of time the administration sounded an alarm signaling everyone to return to the building and their classes.

Leading the students back to the building, we encountered an unforeseen problem. I found the door to my classroom locked, once we got back inside the little hallway. My first thought was maybe it was stuck, but soon found that was not the case. It was actually locked. No one had informed me that once the rarely used door, was closed, a special key was required to enter from the outside.

We were all lined up ready to resume work and couldn't get in the classroom. I was bewildered. Looking around, we were the only class still outside. The long line of students extended to the outside of the building. Trying to gain control of the situation, I went back outside and tapped on the window of the teacher whose room was adjacent to mine. Getting her attention, I asked if she would open my classroom door from the inside. She sent a student down the hall to open my door and we were able to re-enter the classroom. It was interesting that none of the students found the incident to be humorous.

After this unfortunate experience, I always approached new teachers who were assigned that room and warned them to keep the inside door ajar if ever a safety drill occurred while teaching there.

Sliding Into Home Plate

Gaining Approval

As the second semester progressed, I began to receive some positive responses from a few more teachers who sought to reach out to me. Teacher attitudes were definitely changing. Conversations were initiated in various settings.

One teacher approached me to say students were enjoying my classes and the word was spreading around the school. Three teachers, in particular, became much friendlier to me. One teacher in my department, Alice, would come by my room to talk each day. Two other teachers, who appeared to be close friends, would even wait outside the faculty meetings for me to appear and converse briefly. One taught English and the other taught a foreign language.

Another colleague came up to me in the hallway, one day just as lunch was beginning and initiated a short conversation. In her remarks, she extended a much-needed compliment. After asking how my day was going, she informed me that earlier in the year, the coach who had stood outside my door the first day, told several teachers how impressed he was with the way I had handled my classes. It would have been so helpful if she had shared this assessment during that very stressful first week.

It was during the second semester my department chairman actually came to my room to observe one of my classes. He sat most of the period observing and occasionally jotting down notes. Quietly, he left shortly before the period ended. Later, he was complimentary of what had transpired during the day's lesson.

A few days later, while sitting in the science office, having just finished grading some papers, the department chairman came in for a few minutes. I mentioned to him I wished I could think of a fundraiser for a church that would raise a lot of money. He quickly responded he knew of a fundraiser that always brings in big money. He suggested I organize a big "Country and Western" singing program saying that generally so many people attended these programs it was often difficult to find a seat. I thanked him for the suggestion as I smiled and thought, this is Danville, Virginia and with the current mindset in this city, I don't think that type of program would go over very well at the church. This response was good, however, because he was beginning to see me as a teacher and not a black teacher. I never let on that I was amused.

One hot sunny day, an afternoon class of biology students suggested we have class outside on the lawn. Several of the students said it was such a pretty day it would be great to have class taught outside on the lawn. As a science class we could study various types of plant matter. Two students went on to say, if I allowed the class to go outside all of us could get a nice suntan with the beautiful sun that was shinning that day. Several others joined in trying to persuade me to have class on the lawn. I smiled as I told them we might go out on another day. The admirable thing was they had seemingly forgotten my race and skin tone. They were responding to me as they would any teacher. In interesting ways, signs of acceptance were slowly leaking out.

A very interesting phenomenon was also occurring at the end of the school day. Some of my students were coming by after school just to talk before leaving the campus. These were both males and females. They sometimes discussed class work and again they just talked about my family or other school events.

My heart almost stopped one afternoon, when I looked up to see the female student who had held her nose during the first semester as she entered into my room. She had come by with one of my current students to say hello. In a very friendly tone of voice, she relayed that she really missed having me for a science teacher this semester. As she continued to speak she stated that she had learned so much in my classes and they were so interesting. I was stunned, but tried not to let it become obvious. She came by several more times by herself just to say hello.

One young lady whose name was Patty became attached to me and came by frequently to engage in conversations. In later years, she kept in touch.

While in the corridors during lunch, heading to the office or the change of classes, students whom I didn't even know were speaking as we passed.

Signs of marked improvements were definitely surfacing as we headed toward the homestretch!

Although it was noteworthy being the first black teacher to integrate the school, a close-up and in-depth look at the school's makeup helps to magnify the significance of this occurrence.

The School Close Up

George Washington High was an outstanding school held in high esteem throughout the state and surrounding areas. It was recognized as one of the outstanding AAA high schools in Virginia at the time I joined the faculty. Numerous awards were earned at the state level and a few nationally by the school's academic and literary publications. Its athletic program covered a wide range of sports that included football, basketball, golf, wrestling, baseball, track and tennis. It was not unusual for teams in each sport to bring home trophies.

The music program also boasted award- winning groups among its band and choral music programs.

The school set high standards for both faculty and students. A large number of the teaching staff had earned graduate degrees in their respective fields. The student body consisted of some very capable individuals. Many of the students earned excellent scores on the College Boards and other national testing indicators. During my first year, a tutorial program was instituted and run by students to assist anyone who was struggling in one or more of their subjects.

A very active Student Council Association organized and implemented several activities around the school. Student involvement was highly visible among the student enrollment with a variety of clubs available for the non- athletic or musically talented individuals. Some of the clubs for students were affiliates of adult civic clubs and organizations out in the community

The school sponsored a highly capable debate team that was well known throughout the state. An annual school play was produced with presentations given before students during the day and the general public at evening performances. The play produced during the 1966-67 year was, " The Man Who Came for Dinner". It was a comedy written by Moss Hart and George Kaufman. Students who purchased tickets had an opportunity to see the play during the school day.

Extending their reach beyond the school to include the state and even the country, the school was in the early stages of involvement in the American Field Service Program (AFS). Exchange students from other countries would attend GWHS and enroll in the school, whereas, students from GWHS would attend a school in another foreign country. The student body had an opportunity to see and meet these exchange students through an introduction at a school assembly program while others were fortunate enough to attend classes with them. During my first year, an exchange student was enrolled from Guatemala.

It was a very large school resting on over sixty acres of land and similar to a small college campus. The lawn and the inside corridors were extremely well maintained by the custodial and maintenance staff.

There were approximately 100 rooms in the building that included a spacious well-equipped library housing over 17,000 books that year. It had separate facilities for the gymnasium and the auditorium. A large football stadium was a part of the campus and four new tennis courts were completed during the year.

The school's mascot was the cardinal and the colors were red and white.

The staff was under the administration of a principal and two assistant principals.

The principal was highly regarded throughout the state. During that year, he was chairman of the Virginia Committee of The Southern Association of Colleges and Schools.

Prior to becoming an administrator, he had been a science teacher and taught chemistry classes when employed at the classroom level. He appeared to be a very serious-minded elderly gentleman close to the age of retirement. Although I had very little direct interaction with the principal, without any doubt, he was highly respected by the students, faculty and the community. He was perceived as a no-nonsense individual by both the faculty and the students.

The two assistant principals, both younger males, were much more visible throughout the school and addressed most of the issues that arose regarding students. My office contacts that year were mainly with one of these men. Both demonstrated proficiency in their role as administrators. At the end of the 1966-67 school year, one of the assistant principals, Mr. Harrell, left the school and was replaced by a male teacher from the English Department.

The entire staff consisted of approximately 150 personnel who would guide the educational process of the students. There was well-qualified staff assigned to the ten or more departments of the school. Many of these members already possessed advanced degrees in their subject area.

The school had a well- organized guidance department that assisted in scheduling students to classes; a visiting teacher that aided in attendance; a school nurse; a large secretarial staff; a library staff; a large cafeteria staff and a maintenance crew.

The academic component of the school was organized around a semester schedule. Students were able to complete one part of a course during a single semester as in college, and then complete the next level of the class the following semester. This had advantages and disadvantages for students. It was largely viewed as an ideal arrangement, however.

119

Advanced and college level classes were offered in addition to the regular classes. There were several departments of course offerings in the school. These departments included: Science, Mathematics, History, English, Foreign Language, Business, Distributive Education, Physical Education, Industrial Arts, Home Economics, and Fine Arts. Each department offered classes beyond the conventional ones in many high schools.

Each department was supervised by a chairman who also contributed to the year-end evaluation of teachers

The school boasted strong achievement records among its several athletic teams: football, basketball, softball, golf, tennis, track and wrestling

Several choral and band groups were a part of the music department. The school was well equipped to provide a quality high school education.

A Revelation!

It was during the second semester of the school year, I discovered a black teacher from Langston High School was coming over after lunch and teaching some classes in the afternoon on the second floor of the building. I would soon learn that this was a female teacher in the Business Department.

I would love to have had an opportunity to interact with her, but our paths never crossed. Since, Langston was her base school and George Washington High School was mine this opportunity to interact never occurred.

The First Year Drew to a Close

As that first year drew to an end and we were approaching the home plate, I took the opportunity to assess the successes and failures encountered.

One teacher had told me, earlier in the lunchroom, George Washington High School was a small city. "It was large, good at what it delivered, and fierce." She had added, "If a teacher can survive there they could survive anywhere."

Reflecting over my experiences, it was clear major inroads had been made in the willingness of the faculty and many students to accept an African American teacher. Although there were still individuals who never really accepted me that first year, there appeared to be a significant decrease in the number!

Another non- instructional, but significant issue surfaced at the end of the year that caused some concern. A curious situation was observed with the issuing of school year books. That year, the school yearbook did not print a faculty section with individual photos and names, as in previous years, including the preceding year, 1965-66. All teachers were spread throughout the book in small groups by departments. It would have been easy to view this yearbook and not realize a black teacher was on the staff. No one ever gave a logical rationale for eliminating the faculty section during the 1966-67 school year.

As that first year finally came to a close, I found my performance as a teacher had apparently been perceived by those individuals in a position of authority and my colleagues as being successful. At the end of the first year, I was offered a contract to continue the next year. The contract was offered with no warnings or restrictions attached.

I had experienced a significantly improved school environment by the end of the second semester. Interactions with a large number of students and many more faculty members had advanced enough it would be okay to continue as a teacher at the high school. Many of the students in my classes had done well academically and more teachers had demonstrated a much friendlier attitude. The staff, as a whole, appeared to be more acceptant of me as a colleague. All feelings of isolation had disappeared and I now viewed myself as a "true member" of this large school! With these important areas of progress in mind, I accepted the contract.

The major focus of my story has been on the first year at George Washington High School where most of the stress was created and endured during my unusual educational journey. It did not end with the completion of that academic year, however.

Many challenges remained and much unfinished work needed attention. Total integration of all schools in the system still had not occurred and there were individuals who had not yet bought into the idea of having either black teachers or students on campus. Since my tenure lasted well beyond the first year, some of the significant events of those times will be viewed.

Beyond The First Year!

An Array of Surprises

The situations and school environment had improved so much I felt comfortable, being a part of the faculty. Conversations were occurring in the cafeteria at the lunch table. More teachers would approach me in the corridors and not only speak, but stop to engage in conversation. Teachers in the science department were dropping in and out of my classroom before and after school to discuss departmental concerns.

During the trips to the rest room, no one hurriedly left when I entered and the teachers would at least extend greetings, although some encounters never went beyond those gestures. Some teachers after stopping by the restroom to wash their hands were actually walking with me to the cafeteria while engaged in conversation.

Many strong relationships were slowly being built with faculty members that would last through the years.

In subsequent years, additional contracts continued to be offered and I accepted. The experiences in the classroom had become much more positive than negative. Although the enormous amount of stress had begun to dissipate, there were still instances in which I encountered students who preferred not to have an African American teacher.

It became a lot easier to work through those situations or effectively ignore them.

During the succeeding years a few more black students enrolled at the school. Even with the additional enrollments the overall number of African American students remained extremely low for this large school.

Between the years 1966-1970, my first four years, two more African American teachers were added to the staff. It was during my second year, 1967-68 that another female and a male teacher joined the faculty. The male was added to the Fine Arts Department in arts and crafts, and a young female librarian was added to the library staff. The librarian had sought me out and asked me to become a mentor for her. In observing my behavior, she said I appeared so comfortable and self- assured in this setting. She stayed one year then left the system for marriage and employment in another state.

At the end of the second year, I was encouraged to teach summer school and accepted a position to teach two biology classes. One day, while providing assistance to students at a back table as the entire class was doing a laboratory exercise, I looked up to see a small group of school board members walking around the room observing. They didn't announce their presence, but were very complimentary upon leaving.

As my homeroom students moved upward toward their senior year, a couple of students left the system. At least one new student was added annually to our class roll. One of these students stood out in my memory during our sophomore year. He was a quiet and well behaved young black male whose name was Lawrence.

During the course of our four years together, the

homeroom class was relocated from the south wing to the west wing of the building in Room W105. The move, I thought, was a good one because it landed me next door to the biology equipment storage room. It also placed me closer to most of the other teachers who taught this subject.

The school term 1968-69, which was my third year at the school, left a very pleasant imprint in my memory. Two very noteworthy events occurred. Our football team, the GWHS Cardinals, won the State Championship during the fall of 1968 and my homeroom class extended a beautiful gesture to me at the end of that school year.

Having just completed our third year together, the students were then rising- seniors. While relaxing at home and beginning a summer vacation of leisure, I experienced a pleasant surprise. One afternoon, my doorbell rang. Answering the door, I found a florist deliveryman holding a bouquet with a dozen yellow roses and asking for me. Thinking the roses were from my husband, I turned to thank him when he replied, they were not from him.

Tears came to my eyes as the small envelope was opened to read the card. It was from my homeroom students thanking me for the help I had given them over the past three years!

Bouquet of Yellow Roses
From Homeroom Class

Mrs. Johnny Fullerwinder
408 No. Ridge St.

H W Brown

1969

FLORIST

DANVILLE. VIRGINIA

Card Enclosed

Mrs. Fullerwinder;
Thank you for your patience with
us in our Junior year. We'll all
be Seniors next year and you
will really need some patience.

With love,
your Homeroom

H. W. Brown Florist

Over the next few years, I saw major changes occur and
there would be instances in which I would be challenged to
perform outside the regular classroom setting. During one of
those later years, the long awaited event of total integration

of all public schools in the city occurred.

It was during the year 1968-69 rumors had begun to circulate that massive integration was on the horizon. The administration informed the faculty, it was factual. All schools in the system were to begin making adjustments for change. Total integration of all public schools in Danville was targeted to begin soon. George Washington High and Langston High would be required to work on some major changes that would affect both schools as they merged to become the city's only high school.

Just as various activities were being considered to prepare for the coming together of the two high schools, a startling announcement was made to the faculty, as we neared the threshold of the total merger. Two significant people on the staff at George Washington High School would not enter the historic realm of total integration with the faculty and student body, as both would retire prior to the merger. Both the principal and chairman of the large English Department retired before this event occurred. The principal, who was at retirement age, announced he would retire and left at the end of the school year 1968-69. It was his desire to spend more time with his family.

The staff and student body organized a surprise assembly program in the school's auditorium in recognition of his retirement. Since the auditorium would not hold the entire student body, only teachers, seniors, and SCA members were invited to attend the retirement event. One of the faculty members succeeded in getting him to the auditorium where he was presented a retirement gift of a large tractor. Earlier, his wife had provided the tip her husband was looking forward to working in his garden after retirement. She had been invited to attend as an additional surprise. It was a lot of fun to watch his reaction when the large outdoor tractor was brought from behind the curtain to the middle of the auditorium stage.

The other staff member, who decided to leave the year following the principal's retirement, was another male, the chairman of the English Department. He was a very proficient individual, who was well respected for his teaching and supervisory role.

Upon the principal's retirement, one of the principal's from a junior high school in the system was assigned to replace him. The principal of Robert E. Lee Junior High was hired at the beginning of the 1969- 1970 school year. It was he, who after a one- year adjustment period on the faculty led the school into the total desegregation process. He worked closely with the superintendent in helping to develop and implement plans at the high school level.

Almost as soon as the new principal came on board the GWHS staff, he began a series of activities aimed at preparing the school for total integration. That fourth year included some very busy days of planning and preparation for the merger.

Representatives from each school's Student Cooperative Association (SCA) began working jointly to develop a new high school mascot and school colors. At the time, GWHS's colors were red and white and their mascot was the cardinal. John M. Langston High School's colors were maroon and gold with a lion as the mascot. Two faculty members, a male guidance counselor at GWHS, and the male assistant principal at Langston High, supervised them.

After several meetings that occurred throughout the year, the new mascot chosen by the two schools was an eagle and the colors were navy blue and silver. Completing the process allowed both to possess joint ownership of the new products. Other efforts occurred with student committees, which included developing a dress code for students. During some of the meetings, I was able to sit in and offer input that would be helpful after the merger.

The GWHS male counselor who was heavily involved in this transitional process, later helped develop a small pocketsize student handbook that would be easy to carry around. Two versions of the book's cover were introduced. One version of the handbook used a dark blue cover with silver lettering and the other used a silver cover with dark blue lettering. The booklets were printed in an attractive glossy cover.

While students were busy aiding in the transition process, the administration at GWHS began holding a few after school meetings for teachers on race relations. Other issues would be addressed later in continued planning. New uniforms for the various athletic teams and music groups would be among those issues requiring funding with the assistance of the community.

During this period of preparation for the change over, I received a wonderful surprise from the cafeteria manager. One afternoon, she asked me to come to her office then presented me with four pieces of China containing the old George Washington High School colors and design. Since the items would no longer be used at the school, she wanted me to have them as a keepsake. The gift was very meaningful to me considering the fact this beautiful gesture had come from the cafeteria where, at times a great deal of stress had been generated.

As many of those preparatory events were taking place, my homeroom students for the past four years were now approaching the completion of their senior year. Our teacher-student relationship was about to end because they would be graduating from George Washington High School at the close of the school year. Those students and I had remained together as a homeroom family for four years. Even with the many periods of stress, there had been some bonding. I had watched them grow and mature into young adults. A few days before graduation, they surprised me with the gift of a beautiful engraved silver tray with the wording...

GWHS
Homeroom
1966-1970

While attending their high school graduation ceremony that night on June 8, 1970, I found myself reflecting over the past four years at GWHS. The time had seemed like an eternity! Now, my special group of children was preparing to embark on a journey that would take them in different directions as each pursued individual plans for the future.

After the graduation ceremony and teachers had closed out the school year, I was now headed toward the fifth year of my employment with the school. The focus turned toward the very big and long anticipated event- total integration of all public schools. *George Washington and John M. Langston were about to merge into one high school!*

Total Integration

As the next school year approached, I was very excited!

Total integration would finally become a reality! *The highly publicized event occurred at the beginning of the 1970-71 school year.*

During that year, the entire public school system of Danville, Virginia became fully integrated with the reassignment of all teachers and students at every grade level. This was a goal so many individuals in Danville had for years hoped to achieve!

The high school merger involved students in grades 10-12. All students in these grades from both schools were blended into the larger of the two, George Washington High School, on its campus. The previously black Langston High School was reorganized into one of the integrated junior high schools. It now included students in grades 7-9. The female principal, who had been with the school several years, retained the principal's position at Langston Junior High.

There were two other junior high schools in the system, O.T. Bonner and Robert E. Lee. The O.T. Bonner Junior High School, named after the superintendent, was new to the system. It had been recently built as a part of the projected desegregation efforts to accommodate students from different ends of the city's geographical zones.

At the high school, it was the teaching staff from both GWHS and Langston High that first convened as a part of the new entity. These individuals had become the faculty of the newly consolidated George Washington High School.

Teachers and staff met for orientation and planning sessions a few days before students arrived for the new school year. Twenty- three African American faculty members joined the staff that year. The number included an assistant principal and a guidance counselor. This placed a black teacher in practically every department. Another black teacher was even added to the science department. He was a well-seasoned male teacher who had served as the science department chairman at Langston High.

With a vacancy occurring in the chairmanship of the English Department at GWHS, the position was assigned to a teacher coming from Langston High School. The teacher, who was an African American female, became chairman of the English Department replacing the retiring GWHS teacher. A male principal, who had supervised one of the all black elementary schools in the division, became a new assistant principal.

Only two black teachers from the earlier years remained with the staff, the art teacher and I. The other two teachers had left the school system.

When the student body appeared a few days later, the merger process had brought enough students to the campus that one third of the student body had become African Americans. The students entered appearing both apprehensive and excited as with the opening of any new school year.

Total and massive integration brought different dynamics to the school's environment. Large numbers of individuals, both adults and students, had suddenly been thrust into a vastly new set of people, situations and circumstances. Teachers, both black and white, were there because of job assignment. If they wanted to remain employed in the public school system, there were few alternatives available. The majority of students were also there by assignment and not by desire.

Conflicts in this environment were almost inevitable. It was just a matter of how long before they surfaced in a disruptive manner and the proportion of violence that would occur.

Almost as soon as the teachers began arriving near the end of that August, I went about trying to help in this major transition. Several teachers and staff members were approached and welcomed to the new setting. Many of the incoming teachers were aware of my earlier assignment to the school so they were receptive of my actions. I tried to help ease the adjustment of both teachers and students by sharing helpful tips. Assistance was provided in helping to comprehend the layout of the large building and where various resources were located. During this time, some of the teachers expressed to me their feeling of being cautiously optimistic of the merger.

The new assistant principal sought me out and asked that I share some of my experiences from the past. He would sometime stop me in the corridor to talk. This was in sharp contrast to what I had encountered the years prior to the merger.

Upon the initial coming together of the large number of black and white students in the new setting, there was not an immediate merging of students socially as might had been anticipated. It would take more time.

The first few days of the merger were without any reported incidents, however, it didn't take long for a big blowup between students from the two different races to occur. The reactions seemed to have initiated at an athletic event. Hostile exchanges occurred at a football game that expanded into the school's learning environment.

I did not get to witness any of the initial confrontations because I was out sick with the flu. After the student conflicts, the faculty and administration were required to develop major mediation efforts to eventually sooth the anger and restore an environment conducive to learning. A lot of adult intervention, counseling, and some police assistance were required to eventually quell the disturbances and restore order to the school environment.

Two police guards were positioned in the school to help avert additional confrontations. Many of the students saw them as friendly forces and seemingly accepted their presence.

In an effort to encourage a feeling of inclusion and ownership by students of the two schools, a change was initiated that year in the structure of the Student Council Association (SCA). The concept of co-chairmen was instituted. A representative would come from each of the former schools in order to have a black and a white representative. Expanding the idea, all homeroom classes were asked to elect representatives of both races to serve on the council.

It seemed the students chose to elect their best and brightest representatives who exemplified good interpersonal skills in addition to their academic abilities.

Although former athletes and musicians joined the various extra-curricular activities available and a few students joined subject related clubs there was not an influx of new memberships. A large group of students from the former Langston High did not participate in any extra-curricular activities that year.

In observing students in the various settings, especially in the cafeteria at the lunch tables, there was a tendency to group by race. The practice was probably due to a natural reaction to associate with individuals they already knew and felt comfortable being around. It would be awhile before a lot of mixing between the races occurred on a large scale. A few students did, however, display attitudes and actions that appeared to transcend race. It was interesting to note this occurred more among the male students than the females. The positive associations were particularly noticeable among many members of the various sport teams.

There was more interaction observed among the faculty members, as a whole at the beginning of that first year. Teachers were seen chattering in the faculty meetings, the corridors and even in the cafeteria. Throughout that year, a few teachers of both races did remain reserved, however, and limited their contact with each other.

In my classrooms, I introduced myself to the new students, of both races, in the same manner as in the past. My goal was to help them in their educational journey while providing instruction in the subject of science.

During the year, with larger proportion of mixed races present, I honestly did not witness any serious disagreements in my classes. Instead, I witnessed more positive interactions. We kept the focus on instruction.

It was during this transition period, the new principal, approached me and asked if I had my masters degree. At the time I had not started work on it. He encouraged me to begin work on it soon. I often thought of his reasoning and felt he might have seen the possibility of advancement for me in the future. He had been very supportive of me and complimentary of my classroom performance. A few years later I enrolled in a graduate program securing the advanced degree and additional hours beyond.

After the merger, physical science classes were no longer a part of the high school curriculum, but were now being taught at the junior high schools. With the removal of these classes from the campus I continued to teach all biology classes. This meant I would encounter students in every grade level, ten through twelve.

My chairman of the science department stayed on in his position several years until retirement. We became close colleagues and very respectful of each other's teaching abilities. As time passed, we met each other's families and I later attended a cookout at his home that involved the entire science department along with their families.

A few years later (mid 1970's), I was asked by the administration to serve as a supervisor to several student teachers. Those individuals, all females, were pursuing a degree in science with a major concentration in biology. They were enrolled in various colleges throughout the state.

It was also during this timeframe, the superintendent's office began asking me to work on several curriculum-planning committees for the school division. The meetings were held after school and sometimes during the early part of the summer.

In 1972, my own family grew with the birth of a daughter, Tonya LeEll. Prior to her birth, one of the teachers in the science department organized a surprise baby shower for me. The teacher, Joy, had invited the entire faculty to the celebration held after school in the Home Economics Department. It was heartwarming to find the members of my department had chipped in with money for one of the men, Marsh, to hand craft the prettiest wooden cradle for the baby. Lots of teachers and staff members came to the affair and brought gifts. Joy had even managed to secretly have my husband attend.

My new homeroom students presented another surprise. Just as I was preparing for a short maternity leave of absence, the class pulled a big surprise on me.

During the class period, a teacher from across the hall came over and asked to see me for a minute in his room. Since, I was never one to leave a room with my class unsupervised, I objected. He was persistent and replied it was urgent and would only take a minute. The class sat quietly observing. Someone spoke out, "We'll be alright Mrs. Fullerwinder." The comment caught me off guard, so I told the class, I would be right back and to remember I would be able to hear them from across the hall.

When I entered his room, the teacher asked me something that didn't make much sense. With a puzzled look, I gave a response then left to return to my classroom. I don't remember the question, but do recall thinking, " That didn't seem like a good reason to have me leave my class". Upon returning to my classroom, there was a lot of commotion heard. As I walked in, one young lady came up and extended a wrapped box with a beautiful bow. It was a gift for the baby. The students had purchased a beautiful sweater and hat set for the baby. I was really touched by the gesture!

The class then informed me, time was needed to let everyone sign the card. They decided to ask the teacher across the hall to help get me out of the room. He came by later, laughed and said, he didn't have enough time to think of a really good reason to get me to leave the room.

Those two wonderful gestures of teachers and students sure made me feel that maybe all of the stress endured had not gone unnoticed and there were those who were really appreciative.

Both of my children would eventually attend and graduate from George Washington High School while I was still employed there.

The position of principal, at the school, changed hands four times during my tenure. They were all white males who demonstrated strong leadership skills. There were several different assistant principals over the years.

While remaining on the faculty, my career expanded beyond that of classroom teacher. After the merger of Langston and George Washington to become the city's only high school, I eventually became head of the biology teachers, advisor to the National Honor Society, and assistant principal.

As the head biology teacher, it was my responsibility to keep abreast of instructional needs for the other teachers of this subject. Laboratory items were ordered and teachers were approached to assist in taking inventories at the end of the year.

While working with the National Honor Society (late 1970's to early 1980's), I came in contact with a large number of juniors and seniors who were not in my classes. During the first year as advisor, I met a very capable young female in her senior year that had been elected the organization's president. She would come by the science office often during my planning to discuss proposed activities for the group. We worked together well in organizing the induction ceremonies of newly elected members and in planning a special evening banquet for all honor roll students throughout the school.

It was while serving as the advisor, I received an invitation to work jointly with a civic organization from the community. The Kiwanis Club of Danville was interested in beginning a club project focusing on student achievement. They wanted to publicly recognize all students at the high school who had made the honor roll for the year. They were interested in partnering with the National Honor Society to implement the project either through a picnic or a banquet. Finding this to be a great idea, I readily agreed to meet with representatives of the organization to develop plans. Presenting this idea to the officers of the honor society, I found them to be excited and willing to work on this project also.

At the request of the Kiwanis Club, a meeting was set up and held in one of the small conference rooms in the school library. I met with a small group of representatives from the organization to discuss the details. They were impressed with our willingness to assist in making this goal become a reality.

After several weeks of planning, the event was held in the school cafeteria during the evening hours. It was a very nice affair and well attended by both, the students who made the honor roll and members of the sponsoring organization. There was such appreciation shown in the facial expressions of the honorees; it became obvious the project was indeed a very good idea.

The rapport established with students of the Honor Society was a good one. At the end of that year, as the club's advisor, I received a beautiful and unexpected gift. It was a lovely large Pyrex dish in a wooden basket.

Aside from efforts being exerted at the high school, two summers were spent teaching science to academically gifted students at the middle school level (early 1980's). This was part of a summer Enrichment Program for select students enrolled in each of the middle schools in the school system. In that program, while working with seventh graders, I had an opportunity to organize and take the students on several science related fieldtrips. The program was organized and supervised by the middle school supervisor.

Having been subjected to the pressure of being the first black teacher to integrate the faculty of a school in the city of Danville, I felt after total integration was achieved my task would be done. Fate, it appeared, had a different opinion. A period of rest was granted, but there would be more tough challenges in my future. There would be instances in which I would again find myself in a position helping to carve paths for others who came that way.

Other Significant Challenges

After that "historic day" in 1966 when I first set my feet on the campus of George Washington High School, over 100% effort had been devoted to the job. I remained there seventeen years before leaving to accept an administrative position at another site within the system. That position was as an assistant principal at one of the middle schools.

Promotion to the post at Edwin A. Gibson Middle School (1983) resulted in me becoming the" first female administrator" to work at this school. The position came with the realization I would be expected to provide a foundation upon which other females could build. Challenges had to be met in a successful manner. Very much aware of the significance of the position, I immediately embraced a strong commitment to success and to demonstrating a female could effectively handle the job.

There was an opportunity to meet the principal during the summer when my employment actually began. We were able to discuss his goals and expectations. The principal that year was a white male who appeared to be middle age. At our very first contact, he presented himself as a person with whom I would enjoy working.

The school, I found was one of the largest middle schools in the system and the job carried a lot of responsibilities. The faculty, although integrated was predominately white. This time, I would be in a position to supervise other adults. The thought surfaced, how would I be received?

Full of excitement, over being hired to my very first administrative position, I was determined to give it my best shot. Many personal goals were set and later achieved. First among my list of goals was to learn the name of every staff member, prior to the beginning of the school term. It was refreshing when on that first day of school, I was able to address each teacher and staff member by name as they entered the building. Seeing the surprised look on faces, as each person was called by name, let me know it was something no one had expected. It was obvious they were appreciative of the extra effort that had been put forth for them.

Other efforts were utilized to set the stage for a successful partnership. As soon as the academic year began, I quickly became immersed in efforts to help improve the school's academic program. Anxious to aid in increasing teaching resources, I immediately set about helping the staff organize an inventory of all science equipment and supplies in the entire school. As each teacher reviewed their closets and shelves, lists were drawn up and compiled of every piece of equipment, the numbers, and the location. The middle school supervisor was elated after hearing of this effort and encouraged us to continue helpful projects of this nature.

My presence was well received at Gibson Middle School. The students quickly realized I was a no-nonsense individual when it came to classroom behavior. There were many opportunities to interact with the employees and patrons throughout the school year, as I remained highly visible to the school family and adopted an "open-door policy". The principal, faculty, and parents were very receptive and supportive. Many of these individuals, a teacher later informed me, had heard of my performance at the high school. A position that began full of anticipation resulted in a very enjoyable outcome.

As that first year neared an end, something unexpected

occurred… an assistant principal position became vacant at the high school I had just left. After only one year on my job at Gibson Middle School, I received an offer to return to the vacant position back at the high school. A decision needed to be made. Although the principal and teachers preferred to have me remain at Gibson, they did not interfere with my decision to return to the high school.

Returning Back to GWHS as an Administrator

Appointment to the assistant principal position back at George Washington High School ignited a series of emotional feelings within. That was one of those monumental moments evoking feelings of both humbleness and disbelief! It became almost a mind shattering experience as I allowed myself to travel back, momentarily, in time.

I could vividly see myself as that petite, 110 pounds, 5 feet 2 inches tall young teacher holding tightly to my new briefcase as I entered this huge school, alone in 1966. I had come, as the first of my race, to seek a space on its all white faculty. It was not a very friendly turf upon my initial entry and there was no welcoming committee. Ironically, my assigned room was near the rear of the building.

Here I was eighteen years later (1984), about to make a re-entry, this time at the administration level. My assigned room was now at the front of the building. There were reasons to be emotional! I had actually come full circle in this educational journey here in Danville. Fate, again, appeared to be at work. Times had changed!

Excited, but not quite sure how I would be received after having left the year before, all doubts were quickly erased when I entered the school. The administration and faculty at GWHS were very receptive of my return to the staff as an assistant principal. Joining the faculty again, in this new role, would make me become the only female on the administrative team of four individuals. The team consisted of a principal and three assistant principals. My responsibilities as assistant principal were numerous and included supervision of specific academic subject areas, designated homerooms, substitute teachers, attendance and behavior. A lot of emphasis was placed on maintaining a school environment conducive to learning.

While serving in this position for a few years, it was exciting to have an opportunity to co-organize both an Academic Parent-Community Volunteer Program and a Mentorship Program for Disadvantaged Youth at the school. I was able to work along with a community volunteer whose name was Jennifer. She brought a lot of energy to the programs.

It was during my tenure in administration at the high school, I was recognized by the Virginia Association of Secondary School Principals (VASSP) as "The Outstanding Secondary School Assistant Principal of the Year" for the State of Virginia and by the National Association of Secondary School Principals as 1 of 50 outstanding assistant principals for the nation. The honor netted me a trip to California and the National Association for Secondary School Principals (NASSP) National Convention where representatives for each of the fifty states would be in attendance. The Danville School system sent me on this wonderful trip.

The experiences at the high school may have served as a springboard for yet another first in my educational career.

Coordinator of Math and Science

It was while working at the high school as an assistant principal, another "first" position surfaced. Shortly after receiving the state and national recognition as outstanding high school assistant principal, which brought live television coverage to the school, I applied for a position that was new to the school division. The hiring (1993) resulted in a promotion to the central office level at the school board office as "The Coordinator of Math and Science " for the entire school division K-12. Again I became the first to assume another position. In this position I worked with the school division's superintendent and assistant superintendent Dr. Edwards and Dr. Harris.

That move to the school board office would be my final association with George Washington High School as a member of the staff. The faculty and students presented me with a plaque of appreciation prior to leaving the high school, to take the new position.

In assuming this newly organized position at the School Board Office, I braced myself for the many challenges that might surface. The job would require me to work with teachers and administrators throughout the entire school system and at all grade levels. It would also have me poised to work in a large setting in which the principals and teachers were predominately white.

Shortly after assuming the position, I set about scheduling appointments to visit each school to meet with the principals and faculties to share my goals. As the meetings took place and opportunities were made available to talk with the faculties, a lot of the stress was relieved.

Much to my relief, a good working relationship was formed with the principals and teachers of science and math at all grade levels in the school system. Principals would allow me to come into their schools to talk with their faculties during the beginning of the year and many would give permission to hold after-school professional growth activities for teachers.

The new assignment, also, provided numerous opportunities to work with teachers in the math and science departments of GWHS and later the physical education department as my role expanded.

While in this position, working with teachers and principals, several accomplishments would be achieved. A continuous large-scale staff development program for math and science teachers was initiated. Science and math teachers at all levels were able to participate in several after school workshop in addition to attending overnight professional development seminars and conferences in other cities. Money was secured through grants. District-wide K-12 science and math meetings were organized and held on a regular schedule to improve instructional linkage across grade levels. The amount of equipment increased.

During the six years while employed at the School board office, a division-wide Science Fair (K-12) was initiated which drew participation from all schools. We were able to negotiate with the management at the city's mall to display the exhibits for the public. Teachers and principals readily agreed to spend several hours at the mall after closing hours on a Sunday evening to set up exhibits for display the next day. There was a wonderful spirit of cooperation.

Partnerships were formed with neighboring school systems and surrounding college and universities. Notable institutions among the group were Radford University, Averett College, Danville Community College and New River Community College. Science and math partnerships were also initiated with surrounding School districts.

Danville Science Center-First Black President Of the Board

While serving as the Coordinator of Math and Science an unexpected opportunity arose that would allow me to lend assistance to a major project out in the community. I was in a position to aid in the organization of the first satellite science center of the Science Museum of Richmond, Virginia in the Danville community. Working closely with the director of the Richmond Museum and many other individuals, as a science supervisor with the Danville Public Schools, I was able to help bring teachers, students, and parents on board to accept the idea of a Science Center in the Danville area. Through the efforts of the director in Richmond and local city officials who secured a large grant, a Center was established in the train station building. With a hands-on format, its presence brought an expanded appreciation of science and technology as well as added entertainment for citizens in the surrounding area. I later became the " first African American person to serve as president of the Board of Directors at The Danville Science Center". The relationship developed with personnel and board members was a very strong and positive one.

During my tenure on the board, a major expansion was made to an existing building that greatly increased its size. The addition then became the main building and allowed the Science Center to offer larger and more exciting traveling exhibits. I helped to facilitate both the groundbreaking and ribbon-cutting activities for the new facility.

My presidency of the Board of Directors for the Danville Science Center began just as we moved into the new expansion. This resulted in my team of officers becoming the first executive committee to operate in the new facility.

While I was serving as the first African American president of the board, the members displayed a tremendous amount of teamwork. We hired two new employees who brought diverse skills to the organization. A "whirlwind" of supporting activities was initiated. Among the exciting efforts: increased Center memberships, an Open House for teachers, and large science posters designed and presented to all middle school teachers in the surrounding areas. Presentations were given to various audiences throughout the city, grants were received, and fundraisers were held.

A highlight of my presidency was planning and celebrating The Science Center's 10th Anniversary!

First Female Sunday School Superintendent

Leadership developed and experienced in the school system became a valuable asset, as it would be utilized in other areas of the community. It was out in the community, the church, a final leadership position in which I became another first would occur. For almost one hundred years at the church my family had joined, a male had always served in the supervisory position of superintendent of The Sunday School Department. Working closely with the church's educational programs, and the use of my leadership skills would eventually lead to me becoming the *first female superintendent* ever to be elected to that position.

After assuming the position, extra effort was directed toward making significant advancements in the existing organization and programming. In this position, the church experienced improvement in interest, educational offerings, monetary contributions and attendance. The Sunday school received awards of recognition at annual banquets held by The Area Association of Baptist Churches. Trophies were earned for being able to maintain and facilitate good yearly attendance. Working closely with an assistant, a variety of activities were added to the church's Christian education program.

Looking back, I would discover there had been *five* distinct instances in which I had been dealt the challenge to become the" first" and carve a path that might serve as a road for others to travel. Four of these positions had occurred in a setting that was predominately white and each came with its own set of challenges.

Positions of First

-School System-

First black teacher at George Washington High School

First female administrator (assistant principal) at Edwin A Gibson Middle School

First Coordinator of Math and Science K-12

-Community-
First black president of The Danville Science Center Board of Directors

First female superintendent of Sunday School

Johnnie M. Fullerwinder
First Year at George Washington High
School-1966

Awarding Diplomas
George Washington High School Graduation.

Johnnie M. Fullerwinder, Assistant Principal
Far Right-at Podium

Assistant Principal of the Year Award.
Virginia Association of Secondary School Principals
(VASSP), Top-Awards Letter

VIRGINIA ASSOCIATION OF SECONDARY SCHOOL PRINCIPALS
8001 Franklin Farms Drive • Suite 120 • Box K 170 • Richmond, Virginia 23288

(804) 288-2777
VASSP AFFILIATE

March 25, 1992

Mrs. Johnnie M. Fullerwinder
Assistant Principal
George Washington High School
701 Broad Street
Danville, VA 24541

Dear Mrs. Fullerwinder,

On behalf of the Virginia Association of Secondary School Principals, I wish to congratulate you on your selection as the "Outstanding Secondary School Assistant Principal of the year.

This honor recognizes you as representative of the best assistant principals in our state and nation, and emphasizes your outstanding achievement and dedication to education. You go the extra mile and set no limit on the time or steps it takes in developing the youth of today--tomorrow's leaders. I trust you will share your expertise with other educational leaders as you continue your outstanding work with Virginia's children and their teachers.

Again, I salute you and thank you for setting the highest standard of excellence in education and challenging others to do the same.

Bottom (L-R) Johnnie Fullerwinder, 3rd Right
with Virginia State Governor

152

Assistant Principal of the Year Award.
National Association of Secondary School
Principals(NASSP). Johnnie M. Fullerwinder, Center

Science Coordinator, Johnnie Fullerwinder
Standing Near Science Fair Project-Bottom

Danville Science Center
Groundbreaking for Building Expansion
Far Right-Johnnie Fullerwinder

The New Addition to Danville Science Center (Bottom).

Ending of A Long Journey

After a long eventful journey with the Danville Public School System, when the opportunity presented itself, I took early retirement in 1999 to engage in extensive travel. A goal was to visit each of the 50 states. Since that time, tours of forty-eight of the states have already become a reality. At the time of my retirement, I was serving as Division level Coordinator of Math and Science K-12 with an office located at the School Board Office.

Little did I realize my family would remain in Danville, Virginia for so many years and it would become our permanent home. As time brought continued acceptance and achievement, we began to look at our immediate surroundings, and found there were good reasons to stay.

The city offered several positive features that would attract individuals with families. It was a relatively safe place with a very low crime rate, at the time, and the cost of living was not very high. It was close to larger cities that could easily be reached by car. The location, we felt provided a nice environment in which to raise our children.

During the time associated with George Washington High School, I was fortunate to have encountered an extremely large group of students exposing me to a lot of diversity. The contact would include more than 55,000 students. Approximately 6,000 of those actually spent time in my classrooms during the seventeen years as a classroom teacher. My contact had even broadened as I worked with other schools in the system. It seemed as though I had the opportunity to teach or interact with a large number of citizens in the Danville community.

~ ~ ~

During the time spent in the school system, I am thankful for the many positive changes witnessed along the way. The schools are still integrated, adult friendships formed have endured, and former students still come up to thank me for the aid provided while they were in my care.

The journey had, by far, surpassed both the stretch of time and territory I had envisioned at its beginning. The road at times had appeared treacherous; the challenges were great, and the demands sometimes exhausting. Even so, I was able to arrive at the finish line! The journey had been so surreal!

In retrospect, I don't regret being the one who took that "first step across the integration line " in 1966. If I had chosen not to return the second day or if I had surrendered to the first obstacle that appeared to impede my path or if I had walked out the door as the various challenges surfaced along the way, many of the other exciting "firsts" that awaited me in my future could never have occurred. As the days and years slowly unfolded, it became obvious that the outcome had justified the journey. This helped to validate the decision I had made earlier. Having been entrusted with this extraordinary assignment to tackle, in school integration, there would be several strategies from which I might choose, but "failure was not an option!"

References

Sources Cited

National Archives. (1954). Brown v. Board of Education of Topeka, Kansas," 347 US. 483. Washington, DC: National Archives.

Register, The. (1966). "New School Year Starts." Danville, VA: The Register, September 2, 5-B, 5-1.

Sources Consulted

Barnett, W. S., Lamy, C., & Jung, K. (2005). *The Effects of State Prekindergarten Programs on Young Children's School Readiness in Five States.* New Brunswick, NJ: Rutgers University, National Institute for Early Education Research.

Bates, Daisy. (1962). *The long shadow of Little Rock, a memoir.* New York, David McKay Co.

Beals, Melba Pattillo.(1994) *Warriors don't cry: a searing memoir of the battle to integrate Little Rock's Central High.* New York: Pocket Books.

Bentley, Di and Mike Watts, Eds. (1989). *Learning and*

teaching in school science : practical alternatives. Milton
Keynes, England ; Philadelphia : Open University Press.

Borgsdorf, Linda Ann Ruester.(1980). *Ann Arbor, Michigan:
An Historical Analysis of Board of Education Decisions on
School Desegregation Issues.* Thesis (Ph.D.) University of
Michigan.

Brandwein, Paul F. & A. Harry Passow, editors.(c1988).
Gifted young in science : potential through performance.
Washington, D.C. : National Science Teachers
Association.

Brown, Christopher, II   (Ed). (2007). *Still Not Equal:
Expanding Educational Opportunity in Society.* New York:
Peter Lang.

Brown, Robert R. (1958). *Bigger than Little Rock.* Greenwich,
Conn., Seabury Press.

Burns, M. S. (1999). Reading and literacy: Teachers using
reading research." *Teaching and Change,* 6(2), 139-45.

Burns, M. S., Griffin, P., & Snow, C. E. (Eds.). (1999).
*Starting out right: A guide to promoting children's reading
success.* Washington: Committee on the Prevention of
Reading Difficulties in Young Children, Commission on
Behavioral and Social Sciences and Education, National
Research Council.

Bybee, Rodger et al. Eds. (1984). *Teaching about science and
society : activities for elementary and junior high school.*
Columbus : Merrill.

Byrd, Eldon A.(1973). *How things work: practical guide for
teaching scientific and technical Principles.* West Nyack,
N.Y., Parker.

Center for the Improvement of Early Reading Achievement

(CIERA). (2003). *Put reading first: The research building blocks for teaching children to read.* Washington: National Institute for Literacyhttp://www.nifl.gov/partnershipforreading/publications/Cierra.pdf. (Accessed April 9, 2009).

Chall, J. (1996). *Learning to read: The great debate.* New York: McGraw-Hill.

Coles, Robert. (1967). Children of Crisis. New York: A Delta Book.

Coles, Robert. (1972). *Farewell to the South.* Boston: Little Brown and Co.

Crandall, J. (Ed.).(1987) *ESL through content-area instruction: Mathematics, science, social studies.* Arlington, VA: Center for Applied Linguistics.

Dervarics, C. (2007). LEA Improves Elementary Reading. *Special Ed Advisor, 2*(6), 1-2, 10-11.

Duschl, Richard A. (1990).*Restructuring science education : the importance of theories and their development.* New York : Teachers College Press.

Egerton, John.(1971). *Black public colleges: integration and disintegration.* Nashville, Race Relations Information Center.

Ehri, L. C., Nunes, S. R., Stahl, S. A., & Willows, D. M. (2001). Systematic phonics instruction helps students learn to read: Evidence from the National Reading Panel's meta-analysis. *Review of Educational Research, 71*(3), 393-447.

Farmer, Walter A., Margaret A. Farrell, Jeffrey R. Lehman. (c1991) *Secondary science instruction : an integrated approach.* Providence, R.I. : Janson Publications.

Fensham, Peter.(1988) *Development and dilemmas in science education*. London ; New York : Falmer Press.

Francis, D. J. (2006). Measures of reading comprehension: A latent variable analysis of the diagnostic assessment of reading comprehension. *Scientific Studies of Reading, 10*(3), 301-22.

Friedman, Leon, (Ed.) (1969). *Argument: The Complete Oral Argument before the Supreme Court in Brown v. Board of Education of Topeka, 1952-1955*. New York: Chelsea House Publishers.

Gamse, B. C., et al. (2008). *Reading First impact study: Interim report*. Washington: U.S. Department of Education, National Center for Education Evaluation and Regional Assistance, Institute of Education Sciences. http://ies. ed.gov/ncee/pdf/20084016.pdf. (Accessed April 9, 2009).

Gardner, Marjorie. (1990). *Toward a scientific practice of science education*. Hillsdale, N.J.: Lawrence Erlbaum.

Gersten, R., Fuchs, L. S., Williams, J. P., & Baker, S. (2001). Teaching reading comprehension strategies to students with learning disabilities: A review of research. Review of *Educational Research, 71*(2), 279-320.

Glod, M. (2008, May 2). Study questions "No Child" act's reading plan. Washington Post.

Greenberg, Jack. (1994). *Crusaders in the courts: how a dedicated band of lawyers fought for the civil rights revolution*. Basic Books.

Halpern, Diane F. (1992).*Enhancing thinking skills in the sciences and mathematics*. Hillsdale, N.J.: Lawrence Erlbaum Associates.

Hart, B., & Risley, T. R. (2003, Spring). The early catastrophe: The 30 million word gap by age 3. *American Educator*. Washington: American Federation of Teachers. http://www.aft.org/pubs-reports/american_educator/spring2003/catastrophe.html. (Accessed April 9, 2009).

Hirsch, E.D., Jr. (2003, Spring). Reading comprehension requires knowledge—of words and the world: Scientific insights into the fourth-grade slump and the nation's stagnant comprehension scores. *American Educator*. Washington: American Federation of Teachers. http://www.aft.org/pubs-reports/american_educator/spring2003/AE_SPRNG.pdf (Accessed April 3, 2009).

Hofman, Helenmarie H. and Kenneth S. Ricker.(1979). *Science education and the physically handicapped: A sourcebook*. Washington : National Science Teachers Association.

Hornsby, Benjamin F. Jr.(1992). *Stepping stone to the Supreme Court*: Clarendon County Columbia, S.C.: South Carolina Dept. of Archives & History.

International Reading Association. (2007). *Teaching reading well: A synthesis of the International Reading Association's research on teacher preparation for reading instruction*. Newark, DE: Author.

Kennedy Manzo, K. (2008, January 10). Massive funding cuts to "Reading First" generate worries for struggling schools. *Education Week*, *27*(19), 1.

Kennedy Manzo, K., & Klein, A. (2008, July 16). "Reading First" funds headed for extinction. *Education Week*, *27*(43), 22-23.

Klein Margrete Siebert and F. James Rutherford.(1985). *Science education in global perspective : lessons from five countries.* Boulder, Colo. : Westview Press for the American Association for the Advancement of Science.

Kluger, Richard. (1976). *Simple justice: the history of Brown v. Board of Education and Black America's struggle for equality.* New York: Knopf.

Lee, J., Grigg, W., & Donahue, P. (2007). *The nation's report card: Reading 2007.* NCES 2007–496. Washington: National Center for Education Statistics, Institute of Education Sciences, U.S. Department of Education. http://nces.ed.gov/nationsreportcard/pdf/main2007/2007496. pdf, (Accessed April 3, 2009).

Lemke, J. L. (990). *Talking science : Language, learning, and values.* Norwood, N.J. : Ablex Publishing Corp.

Lockheed, Marlaine E.(1985). *Sex and ethnic differences in middle school mathematics, science and computer science : what do we know?* Princeton, N.J. : Educational Testing Service.

Loomis, S. C., & Bourque, M. L. (Eds.). (2001). *National Assessment of Educational Progress achievement levels 1992–1998 for reading.* Washington: National Assessment Governing Board. http://www.nagb.org/pubs/readingbook.pdf, (Accessed April 3, 2009).

Lyon, G. R., Fletcher, J. M., Shaywitz, S. E., Shaywitz, B. A., Torgesen, J. K., & Wood, F. B. (2001). Rethinking learning disabilities. In Rethinking special education for a new century, pp. 259-287. Washington: Thomas B. Fordham Foundation and the Progressive Policy Institute. http://www.ppionline.org/documents/SpecialEd_ch12.

pdf, (Accessed April 3, 2009).

Mallow, Jeffry V.(1986).*Science anxiety : fear of science and how to overcome it.* Clearwater, FL : H & H Publishing Co.

Martin, Waldo E., Jr. (1998). *Brown v. Board of Education: A Brief History with Documents.* Boston: Bedford/St. Martins.

McCardle, P., & Chhabra, V. (Eds.). (2004). *The voice of evidence in reading research.* Baltimore, MD: Brookes Publishing Co.National Reading Panel.

Michael, W. E. (1957). *1904-The age of error.* New York, Vantage Press.

Miller, Lorin. (1966). *The petitioners: the story of the Supreme Court of the United States and the Negro.* New York: Pantheon Books.

Narode, Ronald et al.(c1987). (1991 Printing).*Teaching thinking skills:science.*Washinton, D.C.:NEA Professional Library, National Education Association.

Orfield, Gary Susan E. Eaton, and the Harvard Project on School Desegregation. (1966).*Dismantling desegregation: the quiet reversal of Brown v. Board of Education.* New York: New Press.

Pan, B. A., et al. (2005, July). Maternal correlates of growth in toddler vocabulary production in low-income families. *Child Development, 76*(4), 763-82.

Parker, L.H., Rennie, L.J., and Fraser, B. (Eds.).(1996). *Gender, Science, and Mathematics.* London: Kluwer Academic Publishers.

Patterson, James T. (2001). *Brown v. Board of Education: a civil rights milestone and its troubled legacy.* Oxford; New York: Oxford University Press.

Perie, M., Grigg, W. S., & Donahue, P. L. (2006). *The Nation's report card: Reading 2005.* Washington: U.S. Department of Education. http://www.nces.ed.gov/nationsreportcard/pdf/main2005/2006451.pdf, (Accessed April 3, 2009).

Romey, William D.(1988). *Teaching the gifted and talented in the science classroom. 2nd ed.* Washington, D.C. : National Education Association.

Rosser, Sue Vilhauer.(1986). *Teaching science and health from a feminist perspective : a practical guide.* New York : Pergamon Press.

Rosser, Sue V.(1988). *Feminism within the science and health care professions : overcoming resistance.* Oxford <Oxfordshire> ; New York : Pergamon Press.

Roth, Wolf-Michael. (1995). *Authentic School Science: Knowing and Learning in Open-Inquiry Science Laboratories.* London: Kluwer Academic Publishers.

Rowe, Mary Budd.(1973). *Teaching science as continuous inquiry.* New York, McGraw-Hill.

Rutherford, F. James.(1990). *Science for all Americans.* New York : Oxford University Press.

Smith, Bob. (1965). *They closed their schools: Prince Edward County, Virginia, 1951-1964.* Chapel Hill: University of North Carolina Press.

Snow, C. E., Porche, M. V., Tabors, P. O., & Harris, S. R. (2007). *Is literacy enough? Pathways to academic success for adolescents.* Baltimore, MD: Brookes Publishing Co.

Snow, C., et al. (2005). *Knowledge to support the teaching of reading: Preparing teachers for a changing world.* San Francisco: Jossey-Bass.

Snow, C., Griffin, P., & Burns, M. S. (Eds.). (1998). *Preventing reading difficulties in young children.* Washington: National Academy Press.

Snow, C., & Sweet, A. P. (Eds.). (2003). *Rethinking reading comprehension.* New York: Guilford Press.

Sonnier, Isadore L.(1982).*Holistic education : teaching of science in the affective domain.* New York : Philosophical Library.

Tobias, Randolf.(1992). *Nurturing at-risk youth in math and science : curriculum and teaching considerations.* Bloomington, Ind. : National Educational Service.

Tobias, Sheila. (1990). *They're not dumb, they're different : stalking the second tier.* Tucson, Ariz : Research Corp.

Tobin, Kenneth and Barry J. Fraser. (1987).*Exemplary practice in science and mathematics education.* Perth, W.A. : Science and Mathematics Education Centre, Curtin University of Technology.

Tobin, Kenneth, Jane Butler Kahle, Barry J. Fraser.(1990) *Windows into science classrooms : problems associated with higher-level cognitive learning.* London ; New York : Falmer Press.

Tushnet, Mark V. (1987). *The NAACP Legal Strategy against Segregated Education, 1925-1950.* Chapel Hill: The University of North Carolina Press.

United States Commission on Civil Rights. (1976). *Fulfilling the letter and spirit of the law : desegregation of the nation's public schools / a report of the United States Commission on Civil Rights, August 1976.* Washington : U. S. Govt.

Print. Office.

Vandever, Elizabeth J. (1971). *Brown v. Board of Education of Topeka: anatomy of a decision.* Thesis (Ph. D.)--University of Kansas.

Vellutino, F. R. (2003). Individual differences as sources of variability in reading comprehension in elementary school children. In C. Snow & A.P. Sweet (Eds.). *Rethinking reading comprehension.* New York: Guilford Press.

West, Leo H.T. and A. Leon Pines. (1985). *Cognitive structure and conceptual change.* Orlando : Academic Press.

White, Richard T. (1988). *Learning science.* New York: B. Blackwell.

Wolters, Raymond. (1984). *The burden of Brown: thirty years of school desegregation.* Knoxville: University of Tennessee Press.

Appendices

Appendix A:
Notes From Students

I think that it has helped me
by being in your homeroom this year. I
know that at first, I was prejudiced,
but as the year went on, I saw where
I was wrong. Thank you for such
an experince.

Gary

Mrs. Fullenwinder,
The Best Teacher of Science in
the whole world. I have enjoyed
science this year under you.
Hope to have you for Biology
31 + 41 next year. Have a
nice summer and hope to
see you next year in school.
Good luck in the future in teaching.
Your best student
in science 2nd
Period, Susan

Mrs. Fullerwinder,
It's been great having
you as a homeroom
teacher these 4 years
and I hope you the best of
luck in the feature
B.w.   John"

Mrs. Fullerwinder,
I've enjoyed being in this
Homeroom.   Jimmie

Thanks for
everything these
past four years. You've
been a great homeroom
teacher & I enjoyed
science too!
    Anna

Mrs. Fullerwinder its been just wonderful having you for my science teacher because I th think you are the best teacher I have ever had. Wish I could have you again next year but I'm moving in two weeks. Best Wishes in the coming years in teach- ing for You.

Your Loyal Student
Ted

Mrs. Fullerwinder,
I remember my semester in your science class and now in my senior Homeroom I can truthfully say I enjoy it. I really hate to leave this year. Thanks for everything.

Deborah

Appendix B:
Initial Letter of Hire 1966

DANVILLE PUBLIC SCHOOLS
Office of the Superintendent
Danville, Virginia

~~XXXXXXXX~~

August 24, 1966

TO: Mrs. Johnnie Fullerwinder

FROM: O. T. Bonner, Superintendent of Schools

SUBJECT: Assignment of Teachers

We are looking forward to working with you as a teacher in Danville for the coming year and hope you will enjoy your work here.

Your teaching assignment for the 1966-67 school year insofar as we know now is ___George Washington High School___ science - Should unforeseen circumstances require a change in your assignment, you will be contacted as soon as possible.

The first day teachers are expected to be in Danville will be Monday, August 29, 1966, at which time they are to report to their assigned schools at 9:00 a.m., Eastern Daylight Time.

/h

Appendix C:
Newspaper Clipping

First African American Teacher Integrates the Faculty of George Washington High School.

5-B   The Register: Danville, Va., Friday, Sept. 2, 1966

New School Year

A new school year started yesterday for over 7,000 Danville youngsters.

All but 10th and 12th graders were to report to classrooms for a half-day session but the attendance figures from the elementary and junior high schools indicated not all did.

The School Board office reported 7,037 youngsters were present yesterday morning in the elementary and junior high grades. This number, about the same as the first day last year, is expected to rise by next Wednesday, the first full day of classes.

No figures were available on the high schools, since not all students were expected there. George Washington High School chalked up a first during the day. A Negro science teacher was present, marking the first faculty integration during the regular school year in the city's history.

177

Made in the USA
Middletown, DE
27 June 2019